High-rise inspectors are to keep us living in safety and confidence. Bridge inspectors are to keep us from disaster. Weather forecasters help us find safety from an incoming storm. But who helps a leader from storms and stumblings? Brian Kreeger in his book *The Courageous Ask: A Proactive Approach to Prevent the Fall of Christian Nonprofit Leaders*, asks and answers that one question. Place this in the hands of every Christian leader you know—you will be a proactive blessing.

—Sam Chand, leadership consultant and author of
Leadership Pain (www.samchand.com)

In the last decade, we've witnessed the heartbreaking falls of prominent leaders—and this has had a catastrophic impact on families, ministries, and even our faith. *The Courageous Ask* calls board members, teams, and leaders towards a commitment to steadfast prayer and accountability as they stay faithful to their calling. Though written with leaders in mind, this book invites all of us to build communities of transparency and courage.

—Peter Greer, president & CEO of HOPE International
and author of *The Spiritual Danger of Doing Good*

The lust of the flesh, the lust of the eyes, and the pride of life are ever so present in all of our lives. Even in the life of a Christian nonprofit leader, these can find a home and be a stumbling block that leads to a leadership fall. *The Courageous Ask* recognizes the practical humanity of leaders and teaches all of us how we can help our leaders stay upright in a challenging world. Every Christian should read this challenging book.

—Dr. John M. Perkins, Founder & Pres. Emeritus, John & Vera Mae Perkins Foundation, Co-Founder, Christian Community Development Association

The Courageous Ask is a compelling must read for Christian nonprofit executives who want to avoid the pitfalls of leadership, and board members who want to lead proactively in caring for their organization and leaders.

—Trent Davis, Founder/CEO, Servants, Inc.

As a former nonprofit board chairman who had to guide the unfortunate transition of a fallen leader from our organization, I relate intimately with Brian's transparency concerning a leader's humanity and the impact of a failure. The insights he shares to proactively minimize such failures fall within the scope of good governance for any board. A healthy relationship between the board and its CEO is essential.

—Bob Wood, Corporate President, Past Chairman of Katallasso, and Executive Committee Member of Sandy Cove Ministries.

THE
COURAGEOUS
ASK

A PROACTIVE APPROACH
TO PREVENT THE FALL OF CHRISTIAN
NONPROFIT LEADERS

BRIAN KREEGER

TUBA
PUBLISHING

Contact Tuba Publishing at info@tubapublishing.com.

ISBN: 978-1-7370399-1-4 (print)
ISBN: 978-1-7370399-0-7 (hardback)
ISBN: 978-1-7370399-2-1 (ebook)

Ordering Information:

Special discounts are available on quantity purchases by corporations, associations, and others. For details, contact info@tubapublishing.com or visit briankreeger.com.

All scripture in this book sourced from The NIV Study Bible, 1995, released by Zondervan Publishing House, Grand Rapids, MI, 49530.

To my wife, Dawn,
who has bravely chosen to stay
on this journey with me.

To my past.

The past that informs me
but does not completely define me.

The past that God
desires to use for His Glory.

CONTENTS

INTRODUCTION

I'**D SPENT YEARS** trying to keep up the facade of having everything under control, of being superhuman.

I founded a small but growing Christian nonprofit in Pennsylvania based on a clear calling from God. God called me to impact a poverty-stricken neighborhood in our city for Him, and the vehicle was a faith-based free health clinic. Within four years, we had served over 1,000 clients and delivered over 3,000 visits. We grew to 15 medical providers and over 40 volunteer nurses and staff.

But as I told my organization's board of directors about my personal stumbles (including a three-month emotional affair), my facade was being torn down, brick by brick.

All 11 of us board members were jammed in my office at a table that was much too big for the room. We barely fit around the two six-foot tables pushed together. The room was uncomfortable to begin with. The news I'd delivered made it all the more miserable.

After I finished explaining the situation, one of the board members looked at me and asked, "What part of your issue did (our organization) play?" It was something I never considered. The answer escaped me. My only focus was that I had royally messed up, sinned against my God, betrayed my wife and my kids, and had let many people down based on one poor decision after another.

The board member's question haunted me for a long time and has been the subject of many conversations since. In fact, that question is probably what God used to motivate me to start talking about it to other nonprofit leaders, which slowly morphed into this book.

Leadership falls are far too common for Christian and nonprofit organizations. Leaders have fallen for various reasons: money mismanagement, arrogance, mistreatment of ministry staff, sexual sin and various perversions, etc.

The list of leaders and the reasons for their falls could go on and on. You can probably name at least one big-time Christian leader who fell for one reason or another, or maybe even one closer to home, which can be especially devastating for impacted communities.

I never blamed the organization or my leadership role for my fall. It was my own human weakness. Period.

But there were many facets of the role that created stumbling blocks for me in my Christian walk. Those stumbling blocks eventually manifested in me choosing to succumb to my fallen humanness and choosing the wrong path.

Using the word "choosing" in the previous sentence is difficult. It is difficult because it seemed like one thing built on another until things seemed natural, and all the while I was losing control.

Up front, I want to be extremely clear concerning my thoughts on a leadership fall in relation to individual accountability.

You see, far too many times I have broached the topic written in the subtitle of this book ("A Proactive Approach to Prevent the Fall of Christian Nonprofit Leaders") and have initially offended someone—a board member, a constituent, a congregant, or any other person tasked with holding a leader accountable. I have even offended the casual observer of a leadership fall.

The offense always comes with the assumption of who I think is to blame. Since a leadership fall can be a highly emotional situation, my statement leads some to assume I shift the blame to someone, or a group of someone's, other than the fallen leader themself.

This is not true. Once I have an opportunity to fully explain my position, the person usually agrees with me. So I've learned to properly place blame quickly for a leadership fall.

Ultimately, the blame for a leadership fall is almost always a leader's own. There is simply no way of getting around it—the decisions they made, the actions they took, and the words they spoke.

Sure, there are rare occasions when we can look at a fallen nonprofit leader, scratch our heads, and wonder what in the world they could have done differently. We might even say that we would have made some of the same exact decisions. But again, they are rare.

But I also believe the people around a leader, especially a nonprofit executive, have a role to play in preventing a leadership fall.

Some will call this a leadership book. It is not, at least not in the traditional sense. This book is definitely not a leadership principles book or a book focused on how to strategically become a better Christian leader.

But becoming a better leader may just be a side benefit.

I have read and devoured many books on leadership development and attended seminars on how to be a better leader, how to lead and inspire people, and how to motivate them to achieve "the goal." I have listened to the brightest minds in secular and Christian leadership tell me what I need to know to advance the mission of the organization or how to advance the kingdom of God.

I learned a tremendous amount, all of which has been extremely beneficial. I, in fact, became a much better leader. I always encourage people to continually educate themselves on the latest methods from very wise people on how to improve their leadership skills.

I'm not talking about leadership principles here; I'm talking about the person behind the leadership responsibilities, and what is expected of them beyond their calling to leadership. This book is about something so basic, yet significant, and something frequently overlooked to the detriment of organizations everywhere:

AT THEIR CORE, LEADERS ARE HUMAN

Whether or not we believe it, whether or not we act like it, whether or not they act like or believe it, leaders have God-given feelings and emotions just like any other human being.

They have strengths, and they have weaknesses, just like anyone else.

Leaders can be called and inspired. They can accept love and experience heart-wrenching rejection. They can be strong in conviction and experience self-doubt. They can know God's solid direction one day, and the next day be discouraged with thoughts of giving up. They can humbly, but boldly, experience God's immense blessing and later experience discouragement and anger with God to the same degree.

Leaders can approach life with awe-inspiring humility toward others and God, yet struggle with pride and arrogance. Multitudes of people can continually surround them, but leaders may feel extremely lonely inside. They can be among the most respected in their town but struggle with insecurity and constant unhealthy self-judgment. They can make decisions with wisdom only God can provide then make a poor decision without God and destroy it all.

Leaders are imperfect human beings and part of the fall.

That is what this book is about.

"Your pastor (or Christian Leader) is more than your church leader," says Joe Jensen, a former pastor who now works as Director of Strategic Partnerships and Church Engagement at Barna Group. "He or she is also your brother or sister, a fallible human being in need of the same mercy, compassion, companionship, and encouragement as you."[1]

This book is about helping you as a leader recognize that you can experience supernatural abilities that can only come from God in leading others, but at your core, you are still a fallible human being, and that's okay.

This book is also about how we, as those being led, must allow our leaders to be human beings and how we can examine ourselves to a level that we do not expect them to be Jesus, but a Jesus follower and disciple just like us, with a unique calling.

Simply put, leaders are human, and we need to allow them to be.

So right about now you may be asking yourself, "Who is this book written for? The leader or everyone around them?" The answer is all of the above.

My goal is to encourage the leader in order that they will not suffer isolation and loneliness; to comfort them in knowing that what they are feeling is commonplace and is not crazy. They are still a child of God with gifts only He can give.

This book validates what those leaders are going through as they continually doubt their ministry and their calling to it. It will help leaders to know they are allowed to be who they are—who God created them to be. This book recognizes the courage and perseverance it takes for a leader to continue to pull him- or herself back up after defeat and to live with a constant target on their backs.

However, the chapters that follow are also written for the board members, the elders, the constituents, the congregations, and the staffs who sit under the leadership. In short, those who surround and support the leader, and who often sit in judgment of the leader, officially or not.

I maintain strongly that these groups have time after time watched a leader as they are falling, acted surprised when it happened, and then thrown the leader out when they acted like fallible human beings and not like Jesus Himself. How many times have we, after a leader falls, stated, "I perceived something was wrong," or "There was just something about that person?" If we're being honest with ourselves, we can recall such moments. This book encourages you to proactively respond when you see a leader falling.

I'm sure my thoughts on these two audiences seem out of balance, and they are.

When an individual leader falls, many times an organization fails or is at least damaged or deemed stagnant for a period of time as they regroup. The fall, which normally is of a personal nature, ends up in the lap of the board.

Typically, the organizational leader has the highest opportunity to impact those they lead, whether it be a positive impact or a negative one, so that is where the most focus for success should be.

I am definitely not throwing out the responsibilities of the leader in their own life. I am not pushing aside the need for the leader to continually examine and judge themselves in light of scripture. I'm also not downplaying the need for a leader to humble themselves and accept the advice of those wise ones around them who are truly trying to reach out and guide them.

I'm certainly not tossing aside the responsibility of those who are tasked with the governance of an organization to hold the leader accountable and to act when the leader has failed in their duties.

What I am saying is that many fallen leaders can be saved if a proactive approach is taken by those around the leader by listening and acting on the warning signs of a falling leader.

This book will touch on the responsibilities of everyone after the fall, but the primary focus is being proactive before the fall.

Whether you are a nonprofit executive, someone tasked with leadership, a part of an accountability structure, or part of a leaderships' constituency, a proactive approach to prevent a fall starts one place- with a Courageous Ask.

It takes great courage for a leader to honestly analyze their life and ask themselves difficult questions. It takes great courage for the people around a leader to approach that leader and ask difficult questions when they see them falling, or as a preventative measure.

But, The Courageous Ask must occur as part of a Proactive Approach to Prevent a Christian Leadership Fall. This book strongly encourages its readers to adopt a Courageous Ask mindset.

I have heard it said that there are two ways to address the danger of a car driving off a cliff: one is to position ambulances and emergency personnel at the base of the cliff, and the second is to hang warning signs and build guardrails at the top.

I hope and pray that this book, along with partner materials, will inspire leaders and those around them to consciously take action in looking for the signs and to build guardrails. It is my goal to help you build up and strengthen your leaders and your organizations as you work together to fulfill your larger missions. That way, fewer ambulances and emergency personnel are needed.

This book is about starting conversations—conversations that are long overdue.

To begin your journey here, you may want to first jump the whole way to the back of the book and read the Appendix, which is my story that culminates in my fall. That way, you will better understand the perspective I am writing from. Too many times, I have gotten to the end of a book and gained a better understanding after reading about the author. You also might want to start with that understanding.

The three parts of this book build on each other, so I strongly recommend the book be read in the order it is written.

Now, let's get proactive!

PART 1

FOUNDATION

CHAPTER 1

COULD A FALL HAPPEN TO ME/US?

WE ARE ALL vulnerable to failure: leaders, board members, parishioners, organizational constituents, and members of the larger community. You may be on the verge or in mid–free fall right now. Or you may be proactively searching for ways to avoid many of the mistakes and pathways that can lead to destruction and chaos for your organization.

You've come to the right place.

At their core, leaders, especially Christian nonprofit leaders, desire to serve humanity and make the world a better place. They want to impact the lives of people for the better. For the Christian leader, their efforts are in the name of Christ, so they follow the closely held dictates of scripture.

Every spiritual and life experience, every bit of education, every relationship, and all of the passion they can muster culminates in their appointment as "leader." And they are determined to live up to that moniker. Many do it well.

Leaders that establish a new organization or are hired to run it are full of passion and energy for the mission and for the people who are impacted by it. They have a résumé that fits almost perfectly with the desire the organization has to further its mission. They want to foster a culture that moves the organization forward in impacting more and more people.

The energy and enthusiasm that comes with a new organization or new leadership typically permeates everyone involved. The hope the organization has for the future is at an all-time high. The leader knows what they are getting into, including the challenges in leadership, but they also recognize with excited anticipation that the overcoming of difficulties leads to increased growth and increased impact.

We all know this ideal leader and are inspired by them.

A motivating and empowering spirit is maintained by many leaders and organizations, which, if sustained, can lead to great success. Some organizations remain vibrant and stand the test of time. They have had challenges, but remain upbeat and keep moving forward.

However, this is not always the case. There are also many organizations that experience a leadership fall that causes damage not only in the short term, but they may spend many years digging out of that fall. The leader starts out strong, but somehow finds themself off track, gasping for air. In these cases, the organization is likely to follow along a dark path.

Whether it is the board or accountability structure, the constituency, the community, or even the leader themself, we all want to be part of a successful organization. Sometimes we want success so badly that we put blinders on and cannot see that our organizational leader is moving from success to stagnation, or even to destruction, and dragging us all along for the very unpleasant ride.

OUR LEADER IS SOLID!

A solid leader has it all together. They are confident, dedicated, enthusiastic, focused, and compassionate. They are deeply entrenched in their relationship with Christ. There is a hedge of protection around them so impenetrable it's like a missile silo. Sure, they aren't perfect—none of us are—but they have all of the tools and the moral guidance of scripture and the Holy Spirit that will keep them on the right path.

We know many of these leaders. We respect them, work with them, and root for them to succeed. We put our full support behind them.

Some of you can relay stories of the life experiences of your pastor. Let's talk about a pastor we'll call Ted. He was born in the Midwest to a Christian family. His father founded an international ministry that was featured on television. Ted accepted Christ with enthusiasm when he was 16 years old after hearing a message from a big-time evangelist in the heart of Christendom—Dallas, Texas.

Ted has a true and convincing story of his calling while he was at a prestigious Christian college. His life is filled with many inspiring stories of a life lived for Christ in a leadership role, including how he started a ministry in his basement with only 20 or so people. That ministry eventually grew to well over 10,000 attendees.

He even does unconventional things like skipping the offering and surprising needy people with financial blessings by asking the congregation to lay money at their feet as they stand in the front of the church.

Ted is above reproach when it comes to his devotion to his family. He has children who are always well behaved and a loving wife whom he has been married to for over 25 years.

Ted is solid. He is an inspiring leader. This may even describe you.

Another solid leader, whom we'll call Bill, grew a youth group to 1,200 members in just three years when he was around 20. The rent for Bill's first church was paid for by about 100 youths selling baskets of tomatoes door-to-door. He eventually grew the tomato-financed ministry to an average of 25,000 attendees.

Bill not only impacted people through his church ministry but also by founding a leadership summit that would grow to impact hundreds of thousands of people with top-notch leadership training from professionals and celebrities. He has even written books that have impacted a whole generation for Christ.

He did all of this while holding down the fort in his family that includes a marriage of over 40 years. You know Bill to be one solid leader.

Then there is Chuck, who served with Billy Graham in Youth for Christ. Yes, that Billy Graham. In fact, at one time, Chuck was touted by one seminary president as "the most gifted and talented young man in America today for preaching." The National Association of Evangelicals even published an article on men who were "best used by God," highlighting none other than Chuck.

Another well-respected and admired leader is named Cliff, a gifted 25-year-old fireball. Many see him as the most powerful preacher the church has seen in centuries. Cliff preaches to thousands, with people lining up to get in the auditorium. He consistently sets attendance records, with national leaders vying for his attention. Yes, Cliff seems to have everything, and he is very solid.

And then there is Gene, who faked Christianity until he was about 30, when a life-changing event occurred, and he learned to lean on Christ. Gene holds strong with unbreakable faith through his difficulties and has carried it through for over 20 years.

He's not perfect, but he is a solid follower of Christ.

Gene is involved in every local ministry possible: counseling people, organizing and going on mission trips, leading committees for large events, running and teaching adult Sunday school, and putting together weekend Christian training events. The list goes on and on.

You watch him as he always leans on Christ. Gene heard a message one day, followed up by reading many books, and ended up walking city streets handing out peanut butter and jelly sandwiches and juice boxes to hungry people for a couple of years building relationships for Christ.

Gene was called by Christ himself to impact an urban neighborhood for Him. He even did some crazy things like going part-time 20 years into his career to start a ministry to the most vulnerable as a vehicle to share Christ.

He has been married for over 30 years with adult children and grandchildren on the way. Gene is solid.

OUR LEADER IS SOLID?

All five of the stories above involve leaders who at one point inspired those around them. They each attribute their credibility and confidence to Christ. Many of you likely see your leader, or yourself as a leader, this way.

When you're down and out, who are you going to call? Someone who seems to have it all together, right? Someone who is solid. Someone like the leaders described above.

Solid—or maybe not.

The "Ted" described above is former nationally known Christian leader and pastor Ted Haggard. CBN reported in 2006 that Ted told his church, "I am a liar and deceiver."

During that same period, *Christianity Today* reported, "Ted Haggard confessed to sexual immorality and to buying illegal drugs, which led to his resignation from leadership roles at the National Association of Evangelicals [President] and the Colorado Springs megachurch New Life Church."[2]

Ted Haggard admitted to both allegations.

A once-celebrated Christian leader—someone above reproach, well-respected, and anointed by a holy God—fell to sin and hurt a lot of people. The effects of this fall are still being experienced today by those close to him and by the many people and organizations that fall into the unfortunate category labeled collateral damage.

Solid? The second story above is about Bill Hybels, the former leader of Willow Creek Community Church, who stepped down in April 2018. The same month *The Washington Post* reported, "Prominent pastor Bill Hybels announced Tuesday he is stepping down from his Chicago-area megachurch Willow Creek, just weeks after the *Chicago Tribune* published allegations of misconduct from several women."[3]

In February 2019, *Christianity Today* reported, "An independent investigation has concluded that the sexual harassment allegations that led to Bill Hybels's resignation last year are credible, based on a six-month investigation into the claims against the senior pastor and into Willow Creek Community Church (WCCC) and the Willow Creek Association (WCA)."[4]

Solid? The third and fourth stories above involve Chuck Templeton and Bron Clifford, who, along with Billy Graham, were the evangelistic powerhouses of the 1940s. You certainly have heard of Billy Graham, but likely not Chuck and Bron. Why is that?

Chuck left the ministry to pursue a career as a radio and television commentator and newspaper columnist. He had decided he was no longer a believer in Christ in the orthodox sense of the term. By 1950, this future Babe Ruth of evangelical leaders wasn't even in the game and no longer believed in the validity of the claims of Jesus Christ.[5]

Likewise, by 1954, Bron Clifford had lost his family, his ministry, his health, and then his life. Alcohol and financial irresponsibility had done him in. He wound up leaving his wife and their two children, who both had Down syndrome.

At just 35 years old, this once-great preacher died from cirrhosis of the liver in a run-down motel on the edge of Amarillo. His last job was selling used cars on the panhandle of Texas.

As Pastor John Hagee put it, Bron died "unwept, un-honored, and unsung."[6] Some pastors in Amarillo took up a collection among themselves in order to purchase a casket so that his body could be shipped back east for decent burial in a cemetery for the poor.

I chose the four stories above because of their wide range of experiences. I started with two stories that found two men using their positions to victimize those around them for their own satisfaction. These two men caused tremendous pain, and their victims probably still live with that pain today. I will further discuss this pain later in the book.

These two men used their wall of credibility to separate their actions from their public persona. That same wall protected them from full accountability while they carried out their hypocrisy. There is no question that these two men did great things for the kingdom of God and were above reproach at one time, but somehow, they got mixed up along the way to a strong finish.

The last two stories are probably more common and show two great men of God who fell away. Two men who, although there were certainly victims of collateral damage, found themselves and their ministries to be the main victims.

Unfortunately, it would be really easy to devote this chapter to all of the Christian leaders who have fallen for various reasons, including money mismanagement, arrogance, mistreatment of ministry staff, sexual sin, and various perversions.

The main point is this: if it can happen to Christian leaders like these, who were impacting thousands, perhaps millions for Christ, it can happen in your organization as well. It's up to all of us to pay attention and act.

The list of leaders and the reasons for their falls could go on and on.

You could probably name at least one big-time Christian leader who fell for one reason or another, or maybe even one closer to home.

CLOSER TO HOME

The stumbles of Ted Haggard, Bill Hybels, Chuck Templeton, and Bron Clifford were felt widely, but the deeper impact came to their ministries and followers.

Most of us, no matter the generation, were on the periphery, heard about these men and their issues, and were grieved by the effect on the Church as a whole, but probably moved on with our lives. Typically, unless you are personally affected by something like the poor decisions these men made, you were or are not deeply affected.

That is why the fifth story about Gene is especially important. I believe this is where the real damage is done. Although the big-time, televised megachurch leaders get all of the media attention and their falls are publicized more widely, the volume of local fallen leaders affects many more people directly and to a deeper level.

The general populace engages with their local organization, has been with the leaders to witness— and experience—what made them leaders in the first place. Many times there is a deep personal loyalty. When the fall occurs locally the hurt can be deep, and the feeling of betrayal can be much stronger. You may actually run into that leader at the grocery store where you have to look them in the eyes. I would bet that you know of a local Christian leader who has fallen, even though beforehand they were thought of as solid.

Which is why the fifth story about Gene is especially important.

Solid? Gene in the last story is actually me, Brian.

Everything I wrote above was true. From showing tremendous fruit in my life by being involved in everything I could to promote and share the Gospel, to serving people in various ways, including walking the city streets and establishing a successful faith-based, free health clinic—I did it all. God used me tremendously. And people were watching.

I received awards and write-ups in the newspaper. I was a focus in an annual front-page story entitled "People That Matter" in the Sunday paper for two years in a row. I was on the cover of our local chamber of commerce magazine. I was flying high until I made some bad choices and fell.

It was amazing the things that God did through me. I was a rising star, but it was fleeting. My fall impacted a lot of people, most assuredly my family.

The local, more personal falls may not hit the national news, but they are more plentiful. They are more damaging and go to a much deeper level in the lives of the people around them in their organization, their family, and the community.

AND WHAT ABOUT ME OR US?

By now, I'm sure you have asked yourself, "Could this happen to me as a leader, or to our organization, with me as one of its overseers?"

Yes, it could happen to you and/or your organization. In fact, you or your organization may currently be in mid-fall, and you may or may not even know it!

There are so many situations and circumstances to consider when taking a proactive approach in saving a leader and organization from peril.

The possibility exists that your organization may not experience a fall by leadership, but without a plan in place or a conscious effort at strengthening the leader and the relationships around them, it is more likely to occur.

Naturally, we all want our organizations to be successful. We also respect our leaders, perhaps even admire them, giving them every benefit of the doubt. We put blinders on, assuming or hoping our leader is immune to a fall.

Naiveté and blind hope cloud our ability to pay attention to the warning signs. Then after the fact, when it's too late to fix the issue, we say, "I knew something was awry and that something was going on."

That's what I said when I served as a board member for an organization and we had to ask for the CEO's resignation. I will never know if I could have helped to save the leader from a fall and could have protected the organization and board from difficulties by being more proactive. It is a regret of mine.

When thinking of a leadership fall, we typically think of those that are public, the falls that make headlines and make us cringe. We fear the situation that leads to decreased donations or the disaster that weakens the organization's credibility and solid standing in the community and impacts families and those we serve.

Whether you are a board member or the leader, these are the situations we are trying to avoid at all costs, right?

When the term *leadership fall* is used, these are usually what come to mind. The leaders and situations above, along with the ramifications of the fall, create kind of a street level definition for the fall, and the tidal waves created by the tsunami that are sure to ensue.

THE QUIET FALL

A fall does not have to be overtly public to be a fall. There are leaders who have fallen, and neither the leader nor the organization realizes it because it didn't make a big splash or initially incite anger or a big emotional response.

When a leader emerges, they are full of promise, excitement, motivation, and passion for the organization and their position. Over time, and through some of the challenges we are going to discuss, sometimes they become cynical, bitter, jaded, or they just fall into a rut that finds them coasting.

In this type of fall, nothing dramatic has happened, but the leader has lost his or her passion and, therefore, their effectiveness. Donor meetings become less frequent. Employee issues are not dealt with quickly and are put on the back burner to grow. Creativity and innovation are stifled. Time off increases. We have all seen the signs of a leader who has lost passion.

One fallen leader who I interviewed even mentioned this when he said, "All I would have had to do there was just go play golf (with donors and influencers) and sit up in the office and let it run itself. Anybody can do that."

Harvard Business School professor and leadership expert Rosabeth Moss Kanter says, "Mindless habitual behavior is the enemy of innovation."

While many of the circumstances of this type of fall are different, they can be just as damaging to the organization and should be considered in this discussion of the proactive prevention of a fall.

Considering this additional dimension of what a fall can be, ask yourself again: "Could a fall occur in our organization?"

WHO CLEANS UP AFTER THE FALL?

When researching nonprofit board member responsibilities, the humanity of the nonprofit leader is rarely a focus. But the accountability structures, such as a nonprofit board, a church board, the community, or the constituency, need to embrace and value this very important aspect of any leader.

During the interviews I conducted for this book, I was surprised with how many board members took a strict, business-like approach to the leader. They defined their role as being focused on the job description and accountability in areas such as finances and key performance indicators.

"Since I have never been the CEO of a nonprofit organization reporting to a board, I have to just look at the business arena, and I have a boss," one board president said.

The cold and clear implication here was that the board is the boss and that accountability is black and white and strictly tied to a job description.

The nonprofit board is the entity. As such, the board makes decisions that hopefully will drive an organization's mission toward growth, success, and positive community impact. Boards take great pride in these successes, and they should. But boards sometimes experience the flip side of that desired success.

If a leader falls, whether the fall is personal or professional in nature, the issue often ends up in the lap of the board. The potential for organizational damage is consistent, regardless of the type of issue. Tough, uncomfortable decisions will need to be made.

As I discuss later in Chapter 5, boards and accountability structures, whoever they might be, often manage the leader heavily on the job description and responsibilities while pushing the personal element aside because it is easier and a lot less messy. Yet most falls occur with a personal issue at their core—and yes, they are messy.

The dynamic between professional duties and the personal life of an executive is lopsided and is one of the many things we will work to strategize and rectify in this book.

No board member joins a board with the expectation that they will have to manage a leadership fall. One of the keys, and the responsibility of the board or accountability structure, is to take a proactive approach in preventing a fall, even when the problem involves a relative, longtime friend, or long-respected leader. That approach will include the professional side of things, but must also include the personal side of things as well. As the term *proactive* implies, this needs to be done while the leader and the organization are flying high and blessings abound. Otherwise, the board may find themselves cleaning up a mess.

It's simply not easy or comfortable to consider that a leadership fall could happen. It doesn't matter if you are the leader, the leader's accountability structure, or the community around the leader; it is something no one wants to think about. Even if it might be something we have personally thought about, it is time to start talking about it in our organizations, whether that be a church or another type of nonprofit organization.

The fact is that it is happening all around us, so we must consider the possibility and be proactive in preventing it.

No matter how uncomfortable, the conversations must begin, you must Courageously Ask difficult questions, or the fall might be right around the corner for you or your organization. Let's start talking.

CHAPTER 2

MAKING THE CHOICE TO LEAD

PEOPLE ARE drawn to nonprofit leadership roles for many reasons. Inevitably, near the top of that list is the desire to better the world.

Opportunities in the nonprofit world are diverse, and there is a vast array of causes to champion. My passion lies in the world of human services, but yours may lie in the worlds of climate change, animal rights, public affairs, the arts, or any number of other causes.

In 2018, Giving USA reported that there were were over one million public charities.[7] In looking at the *Forbes* listing of the top 100 charities in 2020,[8] I found that only eight were not human services organizations. Even within those eight there is an argument to be made that they potentially have great human impact.

IT'S ALL ABOUT PEOPLE

People. Most nonprofits are about people.

I believe there is no greater motivator or satisfier in the role of leadership than having a positive impact on people. No matter who I interviewed for this book or whatever articles I read, nearly every nonprofit leader says the biggest satisfier in their role is impacting people. Whether it is the people the leader serves as part of their organizational mission, those employees they feel have had their career impacted by them, or volunteers who find purpose in their lives by serving in the organization, the nonprofit leader gains tremendous satisfaction and motivation through human connections and victories.

No matter how much respect a nonprofit leader garners in the community, no matter how much money they make or how many awards they win, most leaders will list their impact on people as the most satisfying to their soul. God has built this into us.

Even the most selfish leader will brag about their impact on the careers of those around them. No matter who you are, how soft you are, how hard you are, or even how selfish you are, the desire to positively impact people is ingrained within your human spirit.

But although this motivation to impact people in a positive way is powerful, when it comes to the effective leadership of people, it's not that simple.

THE LEADERSHIP CHOICE

Being a leader is a choice, right?

Sure, we can call it a lot of things that seemingly take the choice away: It's a calling. It's a strong bent. It's who I am. It's what is expected of me.

There are also reasons beyond our comprehension that compel us to step up: The desire has always been there. Someone has to do it.

I have always taken charge. It comes naturally.

But it still remains a choice, right?

Yes, ultimately, leadership is a choice. Thankfully, there are people who step up to lead despite the challenges, the pressure, and the doubt.

Some would say all Christians are called to be leaders. I would agree.

First, just by choosing Christ, they are going against a lot of societal norms. It's unfortunate that this is often the case, but it is. This is a clear leadership principle.

Second, Paul, the apostle who wrote much of the New Testament, assigns us the job of "ambassadors for Christ" in 2 Corinthians. Another leadership principle is standing up for, and representing, something bigger than ourselves. But that does not necessarily mean God has in mind for us to be in a role of leadership as the CEO or executive director of an organization.

While this book is mainly targeted at those leaders who do step up to lead organizations in the role of the top executive, I also focus on the various other leadership roles in an organization, especially board leadership. We will discuss this specifically later in the chapter.

Again, leadership is a choice. Even though the rise to leadership may seem to come quite naturally and just happens, the leader still needs to make the choice to step out and move in that direction.

SOMETIMES, LEADERSHIP JUST HAPPENS

There are just about the same number of unique stories for entering leadership as there are unique people. But some reasons seem to be more common and rise to the top.

Sometimes, leaders seem to be born to lead.

For me, the source of my desire for leadership can be found in my upbringing. I just want to say up front that my motivation toward leadership was misguided.

My parents worked hard and struggled a lot, especially in the early years. I was the son of a teen mother, and neither of my parents had a *Father Knows Best* or *Leave it to Beaver* experience as they grew up. My mom was very frugal, and my dad was very resourceful. I watched them work nonstop, and it took years to see them get their heads above water. Oh, the stories I could tell.

My preteen/teen mind also saw other people who seemed to be doing well, but without nearly the work my parents put in. I saw people gaming the system, moving from relationship to relationship, and declaring bankruptcy multiple times. These people expected the same results as my hard-working parents.

When I grew up, I wanted to be the boss, so I could help those people like my parents who worked hard to make ends meet. I wanted to help them get a leg up. I wanted to be the person who saved them and pulled them up. I now recognize that this approach was arrogant and a bit elitist. This approach made me the judge.

I learned early on in my career that being the boss isn't exactly leadership. There are many distinctions between being the boss and being a leader. For me, in my immaturity as I began my career, I had to learn that title and position don't bring respect. I certainly had to learn to respect others and their opinions, even if they technically were a subordinate. It was quite an education over those early years. But I wanted to help people, and it at least got me started in leadership.

Many people find themselves in leadership roles because of their life experiences.

One of my heroes in life is Dr. John Perkins. As a young Black man growing up in the Deep South in the 1940s, John lived through all of the horrors that defined race relations in the Jim Crow South.

John's older brother, Clyde, was unjustly shot and killed by a White deputy marshal while standing in line for a movie with his girlfriend in 1946. John's outspoken nature, as well as his support and leadership in civil rights demonstrations and voter registrations, resulted in repeated harassment, beatings, and imprisonment.

Instead of allowing these experiences to turn his life into one of bitterness, anger, and retribution, John used them to motivate him to work to invoke change. To lead. To love.

In the one-on-one time that I spent with Dr. Perkins a few years back in Jackson, Mississippi, I experienced firsthand the power of Christ's love and gentle teaching spirit emanating from him. We discussed openly and honestly the state of race relations and reconciliation over the history of our country, as well as lingering injustices.

For decades, John has been recognized as a leading authority on the topic of reconciliation, justice, and Christian community development throughout the world.

A third-grade dropout, John eventually went on to amass 16 honorary doctorates, and three universities have established John Perkins centers. He has proven it is not always about education in a classroom but also rubber-meets-the-road life experiences. For me, he has embodied a quote from Tony Evans that has greatly inspired me: "Greatness is maximizing your potential for the glory of God and the good of others."[9]

But John never sought out leadership—leadership came to him through his life experiences. It seemed to happen naturally, but Dr. Perkins also had to choose to embrace it.

NOT ALWAYS NOBLE

There are multitudes of reasons a person chooses leadership. Many of them are noble. Some are self-focused.

In my own journey, I desired to be in control of my destiny, which is always an illusion. The higher I moved up in the hierarchy of my career, the more I perceived I would have that control.

I also mentioned arrogance and elitism earlier. I remember reading in Steve Corbett and Brian Fikkert's book, *When Helping Hurts*, about the caution we have to use in thinking we are better than the people we are trying to help. Sometimes that forms, in an unhealthy way, our reasoning of how we have something to offer them.

Leadership many times comes with an incredible sense of personal fulfillment. I have always been amazed at how God can use something that brings personal gratification as a motivator to spur us onto our next good deed for the benefit of others.

How about the money? Yes, money was part of it. As I climbed the corporate ladder, I was getting raises left and right. As many people do, I justified my success by highlighting my desire to take care of my family. I worked way too much and brought added stress on my family. We almost didn't make it.

It's easy to uncover reasons why people want to become leaders in the corporate world and find answers like the three *P*'s: power, prestige, and paycheck.

But how about the simple joy of leading, the personal satisfaction of climbing up the ladder, liberty and independence, the challenge, a higher level of respect, the ability to make widely accepted decisions, vision, ambition, or legacy? There is a wide variety of reasons.

Maturity in leadership can cause leaders to lose selfish motivations for their choice of leadership in favor of people-oriented purposes.

The desire and accountability for the success of the organization or company is always there, but the motivations and focuses of that success tend to become more balanced as leaders get more established.

Leaders in the corporate world often want to move from "success to significance," as Bob Buford wrote in his book *Halftime*. These are usually leaders who have found great success in a particular arena but find themselves reexamining the deeper question of why, and begin contemplating their true purpose in life.

This sometimes moves corporate leaders into the world of the nonprofit.

THE UNIQUE NONPROFIT LEADERSHIP CHOICE

There are lots of things that make the choice of nonprofit leadership attractive: direct impact on people, helping those in need, deeper public appreciation, spiritual and personal fulfillment, and the desire to be the hero, among others.

Leaders can also find very personal reasons for joining nonprofits, from issues they've faced to diseases and obstacles affecting their friends and families.

But choosing nonprofit leadership also has a set of unique entries in the minus column of a person's decision worksheet. Nonprofit executives typically do not get paid as much as corporate executives—according to a January 2021 study from Payscale.com, corporate CEOs receive over 34 percent higher salary than nonprofit CEOs.[10] Many times they have to manage good-hearted but unaccountable volunteers, and they typically cannot pay their team members market-rate salaries. And the biggest minus for many: they have to raise money, which isn't fun for most leaders.

But many nonprofits capture the innate passions of their leaders, and that is more than enough to overcome the drawbacks.

One great example of someone who was pushed to examine the move from success in the corporate world to significance in the nonprofit world was Richard Stearns, the former CEO of the evangelical humanitarian aid organization World Vision. He had to make a major nonprofit leadership choice.

Richard began a career in marketing for several Fortune 500 companies, beginning with the Gillette Company. From 1977 to 1985, Stearns held various roles with the game company Parker Brothers, culminating in his appointment as president in 1984. He joined Lenox, the American gift and tableware company, in 1987 as division president. He was named president and CEO of Lenox Inc. in 1995, overseeing six manufacturing facilities, 4,000 employees, and $500 million in annual sales.

The process all started when Richard was sitting in his posh office one day in 1997 and his phone rang. It was his good friend Bill Bryce from Massachusetts, who happened to work for World Vision. The current World Vision president had given notice that he would leave within the next year, and Bill claimed God told him that Richard was "going to be the next president of World Vision."

Richard laughed out loud. He continued on to tell Bill he had no interest and was not available. Beyond that, he had no qualifications for the job.

He had all of the trappings of the corporate CEO world: security for his family, the paycheck, the dream house, and the brand-new company car.

After months of wrangling with God in his mind and heart, interview after interview with World Vision, a fact-finding trip to Seattle, and finally after reaching the point where he no longer could live with himself and continue to call Jesus Christ the Lord of his life without hypocrisy, Richard took the leadership job at World Vision. He finally conceded to the fact that God does not always call the qualified, but He qualifies the called.

As Richard describes in his 2010 Christian Book of the Year *The Hole In Our Gospel*, "I wish I could tell you that I accepted this call with a sense of spiritual excitement and passion to help the broken people of our world.

I'd like to say that I boldly prayed, 'Here I am, Lord. Send me,' that I was eager to seize the opportunity to serve. But that would be a lie."[11]

At the beginning of 2018, after 20 years of Richard leading World Vision, *Christianity Today* quoted Leith Anderson, president of the National Association of Evangelicals: "Rich Stearns put compassion over career, leaving business leadership to serve the poor and vulnerable. His Christian faith has been strong and practical from the boardroom to the backwaters of the world. Truly a man of world vision."[11]

I think Richard would agree that the choice to leave the corporate world in order to become a nonprofit leader was, and is, a good one.

REGRETFUL REASONS

We have examined many good and very real reasons why people choose to enter leadership and have reviewed the lives of some who have made the choice. But sometimes people go into leadership for the wrong reasons. And it shows.

I interviewed a successful long-term leader of a large nonprofit who also mentors leaders for a leadership development nonprofit. He credits his success to "working within his giftedness"—a reflection that "leadership comes naturally, is ingrained, and is an attribute given to the leader by God."

As a well-respected, seasoned leader who has decades of leadership under his belt, he has found that peace and fulfillment come to him because he is aligned in who he is and who God intended him to be.

"Working within their giftedness" is a common thread among leaders who are doing it right. They find their life outside their leadership position to be consistent with the life inside their position, therefore creating less pressure to conform and step out of who they truly are.

But sometimes people are in leadership for the wrong reasons. Some of them really don't even want to lead.

Some people go into leadership because they feel an obligation—maybe they think it's expected of them because of their tenure in the organization, or maybe they did well in their previous role. They may have yielded to pressure from family and friends to climb the ladder and make more money. Many times, the leader realizes too late how much more proficient they were in their old job and how much happier they were.

They are just not "working within their giftedness."

In order to compensate for this, they try to learn their way into leadership by attending seminars, reading books, and completing various programs. They're all good strategies, but they're much more effective if those strategies are a supplemental learning that goes along with who they naturally are.

When a leader is not fully working within their giftedness, it tends to create insecurity, which causes them to work to prove they are someone they are not. This alters their ability to focus on the mission and vision of the organization.

There is also the leader who chooses to go into leadership because of a deep sense of insecurity. Leadership is their calling card of success. *I made it. Look at me.* They may even find that they are proving their worth to themselves.

My concern is that an insecure person can sell out who they truly are to satisfy that insecurity through leadership. That is never good for the individual or the organization.

I would be remiss if I didn't mention the fact that sometimes leaders who make the choice of leadership for the wrong reason do possess the qualities needed to be a fabulous leader! But they need mentorship, encouragement, and guidance to work within their giftedness.

LEADERSHIP REALITY

Being a leader comes within a much broader context beyond accolades and success. Beyond getting paid more and more. Beyond the personal fulfillment that comes from the rise to power. Beyond the respect and admiration. Beyond the satisfaction of goal attainment. Beyond the spotlight you find yourself in. Beyond making big decisions affecting many.

Leadership is hard. It is isolating and lonely. It is heartbreaking. It can be confidence and self-image shattering. It can be pressure packed. It can rock you to your very core and leave you blabbering obscenities at a statue in the park. It is always countercultural.

The difficult side of leadership causes a person to question why they are doing what they are doing. They may second-guess every decision they make during times of discouragement and experience uncharacteristic levels of insecurity. They may question who they truly are at their deepest levels.

The hardest part is that most people don't understand the stress and pressure you face, especially those closest to you and those you care about the most.

Some of these difficulties and struggles are so important that I dedicated a whole chapter to them in this book. Chapter 4 digs much deeper into the experiences that rock a leader to their core, cause them to stumble, and tempt them to fall.

LEADER, YOU ARE UNUSUAL

Leaders have chosen to follow a difficult path—perhaps an anointed one, but sometimes humanly difficult.

Years ago, I heard a sermon about God wanting people to step up and be part of the 17 percent. At the time I heard this it was very motivating, and it has stuck with me and helped me in my personal leadership.

What do I mean by the 17 percent?

In Numbers 13, after the Israelites came out of Egyptian captivity, the Lord tells Moses to send out some men to explore the land of Canaan, "which I am giving to the Israelites." That's kind of the ultimate spoiler. Moses is going to have to fight his way to victory, but the Lord already told him he will take the land.

Moses sends out 12 men, one from each tribe. He gives specific instructions on how they are to go, what they are to look at, and what they are to report back on. The group returns in 40 days with their report.

The men detail all of the great things that can be found in this new land. They declare that, yes, it is a land full of milk and honey. They even bring back some of the incredible fruit they found there.

But then the report turns ugly as they talk about how strong and powerful the people are. They tell Moses and his brother Aaron that they "cannot attack those people; they are stronger than we are." They tell of how vast and fortified the cities are. They then go out and spread the same defeatist report among the Israelite people.

The people end up rebelling against Moses, even wishing they had died in Egyptian captivity. It isn't pretty.

Of the 12 that went to Canaan to explore the land, there are two who give a different report. They stick with the promise that God gave to Moses, even though they saw the same things the other 10 did. The two are Joshua and Caleb, and they represent 17 percent of the group. They continue to remind the people that "the Lord is with us." But the crowds are heavily influenced by the other 10, thinking they are crazy. Everyone is wrought with fear and even talk of stoning Joshua and Caleb.

Most leaders reading this have chosen to be in that 17 percent. No matter what your motivation is, you have chosen to swim against the tide, to think outside the box, to sacrifice a part of yourself in the interest of the advancement of some mission greater than yourself.

You have chosen to focus on that mission, and that carries you past all of the difficulties and discouragements along the way.

You have chosen to be unusual.

Big rewards and increased life satisfaction can lie ahead. But you also face a journey that is hard and challenging and wrought with obstacles.

FAILURE: PART OF THE DEAL

I recently watched a video on YouTube of Denzel Washington's 2011 commencement speech at the University of Pennsylvania. In it he says, "If you are not failing, you are not trying." The statement, while brilliant, has almost become cliché.

Leader, you are inevitably going to face some failures.

Even Michael Jordan failed. The basketball legend once said, "I have missed more than 9,000 shots in my career. I have lost almost 300 games. On 26 occasions I have been entrusted to take the game winning shot, and I missed. I have failed over and over and over again in my life. And that is why I succeed." Who would keep going after all of that failure? The 17 percent, that's who!

Remember, you are not perfect, and you shouldn't be expected to be. You have failed but have gotten back up because you recognize that with the education each struggle brings, you are growing. You have seen and lived the difficulties but have pushed through them for reasons very personal to you.

Congratulations, you are to be admired.

But you are still only human. Other than God, you know yourself best, and you don't always like what you see. One pastor I interviewed who is in his 60s, and has been in the ministry for decades said through his tears, "Sometimes for me there is a bit of self-pity that comes in. It's like, how come I am not being used more? But then you start looking at yourself and think, 'Well, look at me.'" He went on to say, "Look at the mess I am. Look at who I am. Look at all that has happened in my life. How could you use me at all?"

He continues, "At times I have to pull myself out of the darker places because questions are swirling in my head about value and worth."

What enables him to pull himself out of the dark places? He is part of the 17 percent and is working for something larger than himself.

A 2015 study done by Barna Group on behalf of Pepperdine University showed that this pastor was far from alone. The study found that 57 percent of pastors are plagued with feelings of inadequacy about their work or calling at least sometimes.[12]

The same study showed that 75 percent of participants deal with emotional or mental exhaustion at least sometimes.

Leader, you will fail. But you will press on.

You are unusual, but you are not alone.

THE CHOICE, THE SURPRISE

You made the choice. You make the choice every day.

Leaders often go into their new positions a bit starry-eyed. They overplay the benefits of their leadership role and underplay the challenges. They think of that nice new office, the heightened level of respect they will receive, the larger platform, the ability to enact their own ideas, and the decisions they make impacting a lot more people.

Things might go well for a period of time as the new leader settles into their new responsibilities. They talk about the future and the changes they are going to make that will benefit the clients and the employees. They give the impression that it is going to be much easier on everyone with them in charge.

Then—surprise!—the honeymoon ends. Problems start coming from all directions. The reality of why their predecessor is not there anymore sinks in. Eventually, the executive's eyes are opened when the problems find their way to their door. They're a wake-up call: the financial issues, the human-relations issues, the operational issues, the community-image issues, the fundraising issues, etc.

On top of all that, whom can the leader trust? Who is their ally? Are they all alone? Where did the board go?

There's also the reality that the leader has to act on behalf of or in tandem with numerous other parties, from board members and major donors to stakeholders, volunteers, and recipients of services.

Many leaders with years under their belts recognize this whole process as part of the deal and handle it well. Many reading this fall into that category.

But there are also many leaders, whether they are newly promoted, just hired, or even those with much experience, who struggle when the surprises are revealed in their new organization or role.

The perspective they have of their position has now become more balanced. Yes, the benefits of being the leader are great, but the challenges that come along with those benefits are more difficult than they initially thought. They begin to wonder why they left their last job and why they made the choice. They were so good at it, and things were under control.

In Chapter 4, I dig deeper into the challenges of leadership. But right now, only a few months into their new position, the leader is finding their view of leadership changing. In all probability, they are ready to face whatever is thrown at them. But today the position is just not what they envisioned only a few months ago.

There are tons of variations to the account above concerning an executive leader coming into a new leadership position. Whether you are a totally green, brand-new leader, or a tenured, very experienced leader, we have all been surprised that things are not always what they seem at the outset of a new assignment.

Hmm. I'll bet this sounds a little too familiar, right?

THE BOARD LEADERSHIP CHOICE

Since this book is primarily focused on the executive leader and the relationships all around them that lead to their success, there is one more category of leader that is also crucial to an organization's success or failure: leadership provided by a volunteer nonprofit board member.

Board members have chosen a unique form of leadership, often based on their own passions, experiences, and missions in life, among other reasons.

Nearly everything I described in previous sections also applies to leadership on a board of directors. The experience of serving on a board of directors is just as varied as being the executive out front.

There are ups and downs. There are successes and failures. There are benefits and drawbacks. There are smiles and frowns. But both the board of directors and the executive should be moving in the same direction, and their motivations should be similar as they work to fulfill the mission of an organization.

I have served on many nonprofit boards of directors. At one point, I was on seven at the same time. Craziness. I really enjoy being on nonprofit boards and believe strongly that everyone should sit on boards whenever possible.

Joining a board allows people the chance to network, as well as to gain a new skillset or improve an old one. Working with a group to make decisions helps a person perfect the art of persuasion. Being on a board helps to develop character in a tangible way. It can be much more than simply another line on a résumé.

People join boards for much more personal reasons too. Some want to be the answer to someone hurting and in need. The board member finds that serving on a board brings personal fulfillment as they pay it forward and give back. Serving on a board may actually bring balance to their life.

Most times these personal reasons for joining a board come from deep within. These passions and desires, along with the tremendous potential of the organization, easily outweigh any facets of the role that are frustrating and difficult.

In my experience, being on a board can be so gratifying. But the role of the board does not stop with all of the gratifying parts.

BOARD = ENTITY

In many ways, boards are much more important than the executives themselves.

The board is the entity.

Although the organizational leader hired by the board certainly has their legal and moral responsibilities, in all aspects of the organization, the buck stops with the board. As such, their ethical, legal, insurance, monetary, and fiscal responsibilities are to that entity. The board of directors is expected and legally bound to duties of good faith, due care, and loyalty.

These factors make the board the organization's true leadership. This is sometimes forgotten, as the board operates most times in the background and not out in the public or among volunteers and clients.

Just like the executive leader, we must always remember that the board member is human too.

THE BOARD MEMBER CONUNDRUM

Balance. Maintaining balance can be quite a conundrum as an individual on a board, and in the board member's role as the conscience and overseer of the organization. The board member has a life outside the organization that must always take priority over their volunteer board role. Usually they have a family and a career.

The reasons they joined the board are important to them, and they feel like they are making an impact through their membership. They want to do their best for the organization, and sometimes that takes them away from their family. They feel guilty when the organization needs them or when the executive needs them. But it's not like the pressure and guilt they feel when their family needs them.

Despite the board member's motivation and ambition, they could also be placed in difficult positions. There are any number of decisions that need to be made by a board of directors that could potentially have devastating results no matter what decision is made. For instance, finding the proper balance between the accountability to a job description for the executive and their humanness can be extremely difficult.

Being a board member forces a conscious balancing of personal life, board life, and the relationships in both. That's not always easy, especially when one group overlaps with another, such as if your friends or relatives are involved in the organization's leadership.

This balancing of board responsibilities and management of relationships, along with the decisions that need to be made in all of their roles, can be just as heart-wrenching as any experience the executive encounters.

Board members, you made the choice to join the board after considering the very rewarding reasons to become a board member while also measuring the drawbacks that come with that membership. I honor you. You are in the minority of the people around you and are to be applauded.

Again, leadership is hard. Both the board and the executive are leaders with their own sets of incredibly satisfying attributes and the challenges that come along with those attributes.

The executive is the one closest to the ever-changing successes and challenges of an organization, and it is imperative that the relationship between the leadership of the board and the executive is solid so they can react to a changing world and business environment.

Mother Teresa once said, "You can do what I cannot do. I can do what you cannot do. Together we can do great things."

Both the executive and the individuals on a board have made the choice to be in their positions for one reason or another. In most cases, they are only in their position through the approval of the other. When they started in their positions after making the choice for leadership, their goals were common goals for the organization.

The more respect shared between the board of directors and the executive, as individuals and in their roles, the more likely the organization is to succeed in their mission and changing the world. Leaders, you made a choice—a good choice—but we are all human.

PART 2

THE PROBLEM

T**HE TERM** *problem* typically brings to mind negative thoughts. We all want life and business to run smoothly. The term smoothly brings to mind positive thoughts. How often is a problem smooth?

The *Oxford English Dictionary* calls problems "unwelcome or harmful," and *The Free Dictionary* calls a problem a "state of difficulty."

What keeps sales from rising? Problems. What keeps relationships in struggle mode? Problems. What causes a leader to fall? Problems.

Corporate culture seeks to avoid the word *problem* and instead uses words like *opportunity* or *challenge* that are more palatable and have more of a positive connotation. *Opportunity* brings to mind a situation that we look forward to, and corporate entities like to see opportunities in fixing problems. The word *challenge* brings to mind a difficulty that implies a chance to overcome. We all love to overcome challenges.

No matter how we view problems or what terms we use to make ourselves feel better about them, they are still not something we want to encounter.

In Part 2, I have chosen to use the word *problem* as an opportunity *and* a challenge.

The challenge is in opening your mind to a problem that you have not necessarily considered. A problem that is seen from a different perspective or life experience makes it more legitimate. The opportunity comes from shifting your thinking to see another perspective, reacting to that shift, and moving forward into a more compassionate, understanding relationship.

Part 2 is about gaining knowledge of other perspectives and also taking a look at simple human nature.

Throughout this book I am working to increase the understanding that three groups have of one another: the executive leader, the accountability structure, and everyone else surrounding a nonprofit organization.

There are problems in the understanding that exist between these three groups that, if considered and acted upon, can prevent the fall of a nonprofit leader.

CHAPTER 3

HUMAN NATURE IN LEADERSHIP

"There is a great deal of human nature in people."
– Mark Twain

"The problem with people is that they're only human."
– Bill Watterson

IN ORDER TO carry out a proactive approach that will help a leader not to fall, we have to recognize one main thing: whether you are the leader, someone in the leader's sphere of influence, or both, you are human. You have a nature that encompasses a complex design of emotions, traits, and characteristics that affect the way you feel, act, and think.

If this book is about anything, it is about our humanness. All of us are human.

To not acknowledge that human nature plays a part in the relationships around and with the leader, including their accountability structure, would be a mistake.

Defining human nature is as difficult as defining a human in all of the complexity the term implies. Plus, everyone has different definitions and parameters around human nature.

It seems like we randomly throw out the statement, "That's just human nature," not thinking about what we are really saying. It's kind of a throwaway phrase. Most people know what it means, but we all associate different thoughts, words, and actions that fit within the phrase.

There are certainly traits and commonalities that many humans share. But when listed, they always depend on which perspective is represented by the writer. The writer could be communicating from an anthropological view, a naturalist view, a postmodern view, a spiritual view, or from any number of other perspectives. And even if a particular view is chosen, each individual has a different definition of human nature in its completeness.

Human nature was a piece of cake until sin entered the world. The Christian continually fights against their human nature and makes that nature obedient to God to the best of their ability. This difficulty is what lands human nature in the part of the book entitled "The Problem."

A listing of great things people do for each other and for the world around them as part of human nature is innumerable. If you want to bring me to tears, tell me a story of how someone came to another person's rescue through their own sacrifice. That gets me every time.

But, unfortunately, the list on the other end of that spectrum is just as long, if not longer. Reports of physical crimes, emotional abuses, and dehumanizing efforts abound. Tales of the interpersonal workings of pride, self-promotion, and judgment are all around us.

Human nature covers a full range of thoughts and acts—good and bad, positive and negative, Godly and ungodly.

My goal in this chapter is to touch on human nature from various perspectives that sometimes make it difficult to see each other as fallible, imperfect human beings, especially those in leadership roles.

This understanding and reminder might be the catalyst that forms a foundation that allows relationships to be spurred on to compassion, grace, and mercy in the context of nonprofit leadership and those supporting that leadership.

PEOPLE NEED PEOPLE, LEADERS NEED PEOPLE

Human nature dictates that we need each other. We are social creatures.

When people choose to live a life of solitude for spiritual reasons, they are typically in a relationship with a deity or something that represents that deity. For me, while not always solitary, that relationship is with Jesus Christ, a spiritual being who manifested himself as a natural human being, someone who can relate to everything I am dealing with in my life.

Those who choose solitude for spiritual reasons typically only do it for a period of time and usually have some type of periodic human contact. Research suggests that periods of solitude are a good thing.[13]

I have experienced times of solitude and found them to be balancing for my thinking and an excellent strategy to get my mind back on track. But at no time in my life, especially in my leadership roles, has solitude been an adequate replacement for the encouragement or understanding ear of a close friend or colleague.

When a person is forced into solitude by fear, by other people, by disaster, or by mental illness, they will do anything they can to satisfy their need for human relationships. There are several movies that depict this that are based on real-life experience, some depicting wartime atrocities and some that share the story of solitary confinement in prison. There are some fictional movies that accurately depict what happens to a person mentally when they are without human relationships.

The 2000 movie *Castaway* comes to mind. It is about a man named Chuck Noland, played by Tom Hanks, who washes up on a beautiful island after a plane crash. The film follows him in his battle against nature and his quest for survival.

Eventually Chuck feels the need for human contact. One day he gets angry after puncturing his hand, picks up a volleyball that also washed ashore, and throws it in anger. The imprint that was made from his bloody hand forms what he sees as a face on the volleyball.

Chuck has now found a new friend named Wilson (which is the brand name imprinted on the volleyball). He talks with Wilson all of the time and treats the volleyball like a real person. This is a very emotional aspect of the movie, and the viewer becomes drawn completely into the relationship.

I believe this introjection by the viewer happens because we have all felt deep loneliness and can relate, even if only in a small way, with Hanks's character. The loss of human contact for all of us would be devastating, and it is something that most people fear. It's human nature.

Assigning human characteristics to an inanimate object or animal is called anthropomorphism. That's what people do when they are devoid of human contact. They cope, making up an object of human representation. Loneliness does peculiar things to the mind.

In 2017, *The Guardian* published a story by Paul Willis titled, "This Reclusive Life: What I Learned about Solitude from My Time with Hermits." He researched the topic and set out to find some hermits. Of course, they were not easy to find.

Willis found one in rural Oregon named Maryann. He said, "We planned to meet, but at the last minute she got cold feet, writing to say she could not risk letting a stranger visit her 'in this crazy age of violence.'"

He found a hermit named Virgil living in the canyons of central Arizona guarding an abandoned silver mine. Virgil turned out to be an "angry drunk" who spent the time with Paul cussing him out and complaining about everything.

Then he found Doug, a religious solitary who had been living alone for a decade in New Mexico's vast Gila Wilderness. Willis writes, "I had the sense that Doug was genuinely content with the path he had chosen, but there was an eccentricity I saw in him too." He goes on to write, "He held imaginary conversations with absent friends, with dead saints, even with the Virgin Mary."

Doug eventually hinted that people stop by on occasion to drop off much-needed supplies, and he would go into town for additional supplies once a year.

Loneliness and the things loneliness can do to the mind can be natural components of leadership that lead to a fall. Nearly every leader I interviewed talked about the loneliness and isolation they feel at the top. You will find that the loneliness an executive experiences, and combatting it, is a recurring theme throughout this book.

Loneliness has nothing to do with the number of people around you but can be a state of mind. It can take a mind to a condition of delusion that finds a person, as described above, in a state of thriving to satisfy that loneliness. This can result in a fall that very few around the leader can understand because the manifestation of that "thriving to satisfy" can be so out of character for the leader.

People need people. Leaders need people. Leaders need each other.

It's human nature.

GRACE AND MERCY

There's not enough grace and mercy in the world today. Can I get an amen?

Grace and mercy are not natural human concepts, but they should be for Christians.

Although grace and mercy are widely known and used terms, they have at their core a Christian origin and meaning. Mercy is God not punishing us as our sins deserve, and grace is God blessing us despite the fact that we do not deserve it. Mercy is deliverance from judgment. Grace is extending kindness to the unworthy. The goal of every Christian, as part of their manifestation of the Gospel, is to extend to others that which has been extended to them by God.

It's easy to say, but not so easy to do. The proper application of grace and mercy covers all abrasive parts of human nature concerning interpersonal relationships. Joyce Meyer believes it all starts with grace. In her devotional book *Love Out Loud*, she writes, "Grace manifests as forgiveness, mercy, strength for our weaknesses, and probably thousands of other ways."

No one would argue that these attributes of grace are needed more in our world and, if carried out, would make our lives more complete. But somehow, we, in our humanness, miss it.

It doesn't matter if you step on someone's foot in line at the grocery store or if you make decisions that bring down a huge nonprofit, the same vitriol can be seen in both situations, no matter the reasons for either. People often spend their days irritated with one another.

And this irritation is not limited to the secular world. We see it in faith-based communities, in churches, in Christian nonprofits, and in our boardrooms. It is apparent in the way we look at our leaders, the ways our leaders look at each other, and the way we look at each other as board members. Sometimes we forget that our faith is supposed to govern the way we look at each other. These form examples of how, and why we need to battle human nature in our organizations.

But when we see the proper application of grace and mercy, it really affects us because, unfortunately, it is so rare.

We might see it in the actions of a parent who forgives their child one more time. It may inspire us as we watch a couple repair their marriage when it seemed to be too late or even impossible. There may be tears of love and forgiveness as an alcoholic shares another milestone on their journey of recovery to alienated and disenfranchised friends and family. We may see it through a fallen leader who humbly reconciles with the organization they "failed," and they are accepted with love.

I am a person who wishes we all had to walk around with a thumb drive containing the completeness of our lives up to that point. From day one, the things that have molded us and made us who we are today; all of the great joys of our lives, and also our deepest hurts and fears, would be on this thumb drive. All of the traumatic events that made us choose a different direction at a particular point in our lives would be found on the drive.

I can just imagine handing the drive to a person when we are in conflict or when I fall under their judgment. I truly believe that if that person were to stick that drive in their computer and be able to search a few things that are related to the conflict or judgment, I would see a light bulb go off, and the conflict would be over. But we don't live in that world with that type of access, do we?

If we did, we would see grace, mercy, and compassion grow exponentially. It's our job and our responsibility to know that the data on the imaginary thumb drive exists.

Grace and mercy, in their proper application, are beautiful things. They're gifts of God. But sometimes we allow our human nature to stand in the way.

HERE COMES THE JUDGE

We are judgmental people. It's part of our human nature to one degree or another.

And snap judgments should be outlawed. We do it all of the time. It's natural, almost automatic.

We make snap judgments based on a number of factors, but right at the outset of meeting someone, we do it based on appearance. Humans have done this inaccurately throughout all of history. In his 1918 article in *The Psychological Review* titled "Intelligence as Estimated from Photographs," Rudolf Pintner describes a study in which he "investigated the relationship between people's snap judgments about the intelligence of children from their appearance, and the actual intelligence scores of these children."

The study gathered together groups of physicians, psychologists, students, and teachers. These groups were shown pictures of 12 children who were ranked using the Yerkes-Bridge Scale and were ranked from very bright to feeble-minded. The ranking by the groups of intelligence as based on appearance ranked very poorly. The study concluded that appearance is not a good indicator of intelligence.

I chose to use this study from the early 1900s to show the persistence and stubbornness of basic human nature. This is one study of many that shows human nature rarely changes.

But we go on making judgments, especially snap judgments, don't we? It's human nature.

Someone cuts you off in traffic, and all of a sudden, everything about the situation falls under judgment: the car they are driving, the upbringing and character of the driver, what the driver looks like, the cars around the incident, and the weather. It goes on and on. But you usually hear, "I did nothing wrong!" (Anyone who has a teenage driver in their household understands this clearly. My son rear-ended three different vehicles in three different incidents, but it was always the other driver's fault?!)

And it's no different in church. Week after week, the same family with three children walks into church late, causing a commotion, and everything about them falls under judgment.: "What kind of parents are they? Look at the irresponsibility they are teaching their children. Surely, they could have gotten up earlier. What kind of parents were their parents?" And then it hits spiritually: "I was really hearing God speak to me when they walked in late. When they come in late, it really creates a stumbling block for me."

We tend to do the same to our leaders: "Why are they taking the ministry in that direction? Did you hear what they just said? What do they do all day? Look at the car they drive. Is that a tattoo? How can they afford that house?" "I hear *(fill in the blank with gossip)*. —They did what? How do they still have a job?" And, of course, we get scriptural: "You know, they are just not being a good steward. I thought the body is the temple of the Holy Spirit. Pride comes before the fall."

A number of studies and articles published in journals indicate that judgments of people usually fall into three categories: morality, competence, and sociability.[14]

Judgment of morality affects how we think of the other two. For instance, there may be someone you work with who is an incredibly social person who does a great job. But if you sense that there just isn't something right with them morally, you are less likely to trust them socially, or you may doubt their competency.

Scripture is full of examples of improper judgment and cautions us against it repeatedly. God clearly wants us to apply compassion and understanding to others and always wants us to take the high road, especially when we don't have all of the facts or don't have the full context of a situation.

Have you heard the phrase, "If any one of you is without sin, let him be the first to throw a stone" (John 8:7)? In the first and second verses of Matthew 7, we read, "Do not judge, or you too will be judged. For in the same way you judge others, you will be judged, and with the measure you use, it will be measured to you." And right below it, in Matthew 7:3, we find, "Why do you look at the speck of sawdust in your brother's eye and pay no attention to the plank in your own eye?"

Just like the off-track Christian leader, it is hard to take that word that we hold so dear and get it from our heads to our hearts where the rubber meets the road. But we *can* do it, and we must.

I strongly believe that judgment of the world around us and the people in it is part of the deal of our existence here, part of human nature. The key is how hard we battle those judgments as part of human nature when we deem them immoral, inappropriate, or incongruent with what we believe from a spiritual perspective or who we are. And we need to fight hard to bring those judgments in line.

One of the most dangerous, and most times inaccurate, judgments we tend to make is the judgment of someone's motives.

ASSUMED MOTIVES

"The board made that decision because they want to see me fail."

"The executive said that during his speech because they want the board to look stupid and uncooperative."

"My spouse said that because they want me to look bad in front of the kids, so they can run the house."

"My parents made me stay home Friday night because they don't want me to be popular."

"My boss did that because they want to hold me back."

These are all examples of how we judge the motives of others. When you really think about it, how much of this judgment is actually based on the person we are judging? Sure, there may be some things from the past concerning the person that take you down a particular path, but I would suspect that most of what a person is basing their judgment on is their own life experience, their unique perspective.

The presumed motive a person comes up with can either be positive or negative. My experience has shown me that the direction of a judgment of motives is based more on the person making the judgment than the person being judged. If the person making the judgment has a generally rosy view of life and people, the motive will be judged as positive and beneficial with good intentions. But if the person making the judgment has a sour outlook on life and people, the motive will most likely be judged as negative, devious, and perhaps manipulative.

Unfortunately, the latter happens way too often.

Many times this happens because of a lack of communication and relationship between leaders and others connected to the organization. As with many parts of human nature that can be potentially damaging to the board-leader relationship, judging motives on both ends can possibly be completely averted with increased communication.

"Over the years I have noticed that one of the chief ways people get into trouble with one another is by judging motives."[15] Those are the words of Dr. Jay Adams of the Institute for Nouthetic Studies. For almost 50 years, he was at the forefront of a movement calling pastors and other Christian workers back to the scriptures in their counseling ministries.

He goes on to say, "How seldom do we admit we are only guessing and do not really know what is going on in someone else's mind. We think and act as though we have the ability to read minds, but the fact is, we don't. The ability to read minds and motives belongs to God alone."

But we tend to think we can surmise another's motives, don't we?

The chances we are going to accurately determine someone's motives as part of a snap judgment are low. But that is what we typically do, especially with our leaders.

Dr. Adams writes that "until the evidence proves otherwise, we are to make the loving interpretation of another's words or actions, always giving him or her the benefit of every doubt: 'Love... believes all things, hopes all things' (1 Cor. 13:7)."

It is the rare person that can do this off the cuff. I hope that person is you. Another battle against human nature.

PSYCHOLOGICALLY SPEAKING

In the world of psychology there is a term called fundamental attribution error (FAE, also known as correspondence bias or over-attribution effect). Psychologist Lee Ross, who coined the term in the 1980s, defined it as "a tendency for people, when attributing the causes of behavior, to underestimate the impact of situational factors and to overestimate the role of dispositional factors in controlling behavior."[16]

Put in plainer language, Scott McGreal, in an article for *Psychology Today*, writes that this means "even when someone has very little choice in how they behave because of external environmental demands (i.e., situational factors controlled their behavior), other people tend to assume that they behaved the way they did because of their own attributes, such as their personality, attitudes, and desires (i.e., dispositional factors)."[17]

The reality is, sometimes the reason we do something is because of a temporary circumstance and is not necessarily tied to who we deeply are.

No matter whose definition you use or understand better, this is part of human nature.

Psychologist Mark Sherman, also in *Psychology Today*, writes, "Interestingly, social psychologists have found that we make the fundamental attribution error (FAE) about other people but rarely ourselves. When we do things, we always have a good reason. It's other people we see as defective. (FAE or not, other people are defective. If everyone was more like me, this world would be a much better place!)."[18]

And then on the other side of the spectrum, but related, you have self-serving bias. The self-serving bias is defined as people's tendency to attribute positive events to their own character but attribute negative events to external factors. It's a common type of cognitive bias that has been extensively studied in social psychology.[19]

Here are a few examples: Remember my son, the teenage driver who early on rear-ended three cars but never took the blame? He would always talk about what a good driver he was and attributed it to his natural ability. But when he was in an accident, there was always another reason outside himself. So, when you get an A on a paper it is because you prepared correctly and have the natural intelligence to achieve the grade, but when you get a C on the next paper in the same class, it's the instructor's fault?

Does this sound familiar? I'll bet it does.

Whether it is FAE, attribution bias, or any one of a number of psychological principles, these biases and tendencies are alive and well, especially when we are looking at our leaders.

Think of how these attributes of human nature come alive in a boardroom. Remember, the board members and the leaders all have biases.

But we sometimes forget. These things come into play when the board members look at each other, when the board looks at the leader, and when the leader looks at the board.

Human nature is a battle. It is a battle that must be fought if we are going to proactively work to prevent the fall of a nonprofit leader.

FEAR OF LOOKING BAD (FOLB)

No one wants to look bad.

What others think of us is important, regardless of what people may say. Sure, many people say they don't care what others think of them, but when push comes to shove, they protect their image just like everyone else.

We do everything we can to protect the image we have of ourselves and how others view us, sometimes to the detriment of others.

It is human nature to desire to be thought well of.

FOLB causes us to be hesitant and doubt ourselves, to stretch the truth, to apologize too much, to be afraid to share our opinion, to step outside the box, to dare, etc.

I have a large magnet on my refrigerator that says, "Life begins at the end of your comfort zone." The magnet reminds me to avoid placing limits on my potential based on fear.

Believe me, I have done a lot of stupid things and made a fool of myself numerous times. But I have also experienced joy, unbridled success, and things that most will never experience because I was not afraid of looking bad. Writing this book alone is a big risk.

Think about how this plays out in the boardroom or nonprofit leadership. The nonprofit leader may not want to risk looking bad to their family, the board, the community, or their constituency. This may stifle innovation and creativity.

The board may have similar fears of looking bad. And this fear tends to skew our judgment in matters of decision-making and governance.

This fear causes leaders to hide struggles from view in order to protect their image. Although the leader may think they are protecting their image and the image of the organization, many times they are prolonging the inevitable, which will tarnish the leader and organization to a much higher level. We are going to travel through this in future chapters, so hang in there.

In her very inspiring song "This Journey Is My Own," Christian artist Sara Groves sings, "And now I live and I breathe for an audience of One."

That audience of One does not currently have flesh, but trying to please the flesh is part of the human nature we battle, whether it is in our personal lives, in our society, or in the boardroom.

THE LAND OF ASSUMPTION

When we are judgmental without all of the information, we typically find ourselves in the land of assumption. In the land of assumption, we find things that are accepted as true or as certain to happen, but without proof. And taking assumptions as fact can lead us down the wrong path.

Henry Winkler (yes, The Fonz) said, "Assumptions are the termites of relationships."

Instead of operating on assumption, Courageously Ask. Communicate. Just like in a healthy, long-term marriage, solid, transparent communication between a leader and their accountability structure is vital.

This isn't always easy in this day and age, as we find ourselves beholden to the text message, email, and social media—communication that is easy to misconstrue and often fails to capture necessary context.

Many modern modes of communication simply cannot capture the numerous forms of nonverbal communication.

Albert Mehrabian, professor emeritus of psychology at UCLA, is known for his breakdown of human communication into the following: 7 percent spoken words, 38 percent tone of voice, and 55 percent body language. While some disagree on those numbers, it's indisputable that nonverbal communication dominates verbal.

So if we are continually relying on modes of communication only containing words in written form, research shows that we are missing a large majority of the message being communicated. When we miss a large majority of the communication, human nature typically sends us to the land of assumption where tension, conflict, and uninformed decisions reside.

It doesn't matter if there is conflict between the board and leader, if there is conflict among board members, or if there are assumptions among staff creating drama—increased communication to gain information almost always provides a ticket out of the land of assumption.

People, especially leaders, need to have the courage to ask the difficult questions. The answer to an unasked question could be the key to increased understanding and relationship, but we have to push aside the temptation to assume in order to ask the question. Without that answer there could be increased drama that plants a seed of doubt in a leader or a board member. That seed could grow to accusations or maybe even a fall.

Sometimes we have to fight human nature and assume the best until we have all of the facts. But we have to pay attention and ask.

TMI

I am naturally a news junkie. So much so that it starts to consume me. It's on my radio, on my television, and on my phone. I still purchase a Sunday paper. For most of my adult life, the first activity of my day has been reading the morning paper.

I'm not sure I can perfectly answer why that is, but I do know that I always want to be on the cusp of anything that happens, especially politically.

I want to attempt to be the most informed person in the room.

Interpersonal relationships are my thing, and when you are well-informed, you can talk to almost anyone. My wife says I can make friends with a brick wall, and I attribute much of that to being well-informed.

I find that many leaders desire to be well-informed. They want to stay on top of their game.

But I've come to realize that being well-informed by watching TV, listening to the radio, and reading news on my phone really hurts my outlook on the world. It hurts my outlook on people. Information addiction makes me skeptical of people and organizations. I'm sometimes cynical. It even skews what I think about myself.

And a generally negative outlook on the world and people, skepticism, and cynicism don't exactly help me as a leader. They tend to steal joy and motivation.

The news attempts to share wonderful stories about people doing great things. But let's be honest; by and large, the news shares the worst of the human condition, and for some reason many of us are attracted to it. Human nature?

In today's world, the negative news is seemingly constant. It never ends. Political, entertainment, sports, business, even nonprofit—there is always a scandal somewhere revealing the worst in human nature.

Evidence that humans prefer negative news to positive news is very well documented. For instance, a 2019 study by the Proceedings of the National Academy of Sciences of the United States of America (PNAS) of over 1,000 respondents across 17 countries and six continents reported, "Researchers note the great significance of these findings, which suggest that people all around the world react more strongly to negative news content. While journalists are responsible for producing more negative news, it could be that consumers are demanding it, consciously or not."[20]

And negative news affects the way we think about the world and those around us. Dr. Austin Perlmutter writes that "while negative news may influence our thinking through multiple mechanisms, one important consideration is how it interfaces with our cognitive biases, keeping our focus on everything that's going wrong while blinding us to all the good things around us."[21]

There is a clear appeal to the negative side of human nature.

People do not get a fair shot at showing their goodness because I have built up a perception of humanity, and I apply it to every person I meet through judgments I make about them. Sometimes it is positive, but if I'm honest, many times it is not. Whether it is the way they look, the way they dress, or the way they talk, it is always a snap judgment based on inaccurate information, most times before they open their mouth.

The ability to measure the influence the news or any other source of information has on our judgment is extremely important. This can definitely come into play as we navigate the relationships within a nonprofit, or any workplace for that matter.

When making important decisions or making difficult judgments, it is important that our minds are free from outside influences so we can make wise, well-informed decisions. This is difficult and sometimes on the edge of the subconscious, but it is something we must be careful of.

I did an exercise that I credit to Tim Ferris and his book *The 4-Hour Workweek*. I went on an information fast and turned off the news. Everything that would bring me current news and information was turned off for one week. He even encouraged backing down on nonfiction reading.

I was amazed at how my outlook changed and how little of the missing information I actually needed. Hardly anything changed in the world around me. It was like picking up a TV program you haven't watched for a season only to find that you barely missed anything.

My thinking seemed clearer and less clouded. I looked at people differently. I looked at myself differently. The negative, judgmental thoughts subsided for the most part. I was much more productive. Yes, in just one week.

I now do information fasts regularly and for longer periods of time.

But one question always remains: does the problem lie in the media, or are they just revealing and yielding to human nature?

Another area that causes us to gain too much information, which many times is inaccurate, is gossip.

A 2020 story by journalist Lauren Kent revealed, "Social scientists have found that everyone is hardwired to pay attention to gossip, and to participate in it. In fact, it's an evolutionary adaptation—it's become human nature to spill the tea."[22]

Gossip is part of human nature. Desiring more and more information is human nature. For too many people, seeking negative information is human nature. And don't even get me started on the misuse of the Internet!

There is a ton of information out there for us to manage and make sure it is accurate. It is our responsibility—another battle of human nature. This is especially important when we are attempting to be a positive force in the support of leadership in a nonprofit setting.

We are judgmental people. We are our own number one fan. We can always justify the things we do. We always give ourselves a break—the breaks we aren't willing to give others. We are critical of others when we see ourselves doing the same things.

As Christians, we usually know the scripture or principle, but struggle to apply it. We always think we should receive grace and mercy, but hesitate to give it to others.

We want people to draw a line and forgive and forget, but justify why we can't do the same.

We understand the context of our life, but don't seek to know the same from others. We want to have friends, but don't want to be a friend. We criticize leadership, but balk at the opportunity to become one. We battle when what we really need to do is surrender. The list of relational challenges as part of human nature goes on and on.

This is who we are naturally, but it's a battle we must fight. And some people do it very well. Although it was difficult to complete the list above and not feel completely cynical, I can think of so many inspiring stories where people have overcome human nature.

Yes, many of us desire to do great things and impact as many people as possible in helping to improve their lives. I like to think I am part of this group but find myself wandering into the negative side of human nature way too often.

As leaders we make it happen, God smiles down on us, and the world is a better place because we are in it. No question.

But there is no denying what I described above, and it all needs to be considered when we are developing relationships that will proactively support a leader in order to avoid a fall.

Keep in mind, I have only touched on human nature in this chapter.

I bring these things up now in this section because the battle against human nature is one of the most important things that can happen in the boardroom of a Christian nonprofit. Each positive story that I hear concerning the relationship between a board and leader in a Christian nonprofit starts with both parties humbly recognizing the need for supernatural intervention and the need to consciously battle human nature.

This successful battle against human nature and not just relying on, but consciously allowing God to intervene is an absolute key in the success of a Christian nonprofit.

CHAPTER 4

STRUGGLES AT THE TOP

IN THIS CHAPTER I use my personal experience, many interviews, and research to lay out some of the common struggles leaders, especially executives, deal with. These struggles can turn into stumbling blocks, which can turn into temptation, sometimes manifest in sin, and eventually can end up as a fall.

They did with me.

KNOWN, LOVED, ACCEPTED. WHO?

"To be loved but not known is comforting but superficial. To be known and not loved is our greatest fear. But to be fully known and truly loved is, well, a lot like being loved by God. It is what we need more than anything. It liberates us from pretense, humbles us out of our self-righteousness, and fortifies us for any difficulty life can throw at us." These are the words of Tim Keller in his book *The Meaning of Marriage*.

A closer look at what the love Keller is speaking of includes being fully known to our deepest levels, by at least one person, and to still be accepted and loved without condition and without judgment. That's the love God provides for us and the love we are to provide to others.

Stop for a second and think about what you just read. How hard is that?

How hard is that, not just for the person sharing themself but for the giver of the love and acceptance? The person sharing has to get past the natural human fear of not being accepted, and the person being shared with has to withhold judgment and love unconditionally. Neither is easy.

As part of human nature, each of us has a place within ourselves we will always conceal. Usually this comes down to fear of one thing or another. A leader has to be able to reveal to a level only they can determine. Hopefully, all of us care enough about our leaders that we are always gently pushing those boundaries and also pushing our own boundaries of love and acceptance of them.

This all forms a backdrop for what I believe to be the number one reason Christian leaders find themselves ineffective and/or eventually fall.

I have spent time with secular nonprofit leaders, Christian leaders, and many pastors over the years, and have asked them the question, "Do you have anyone in your life, other than God Himself, to whom you can allow yourself to be fully known?" I'm not talking about a common accountability partner. What I am talking about goes much deeper.

Usually, the answer right off the bat is yes, and they tell me about the person.

But then I challenge them with some possibly ugly parts of ourselves, with examples of ugliness that might be in our lives—the stuff we keep in the deepest, darkest parts of ourselves- the stuff that may change the person's view of them.

It's extremely rare that someone has this person, but it exists sometimes.

Occasionally, someone will answer with, "My spouse." It rarely takes but one or two examples for that one to be blown out of the water.

I may ask, "So if you have a pornography issue or are attracted to someone in the office, you can take it to your spouse?" This is where the leader almost always changes their tune, and the atmosphere becomes a little more somber.

At this point they have to consider the totality of themselves. Many times, this is where they get uncomfortable, sometimes even defensive. Sometimes they think I am judging them, not recognizing that I am dealing with the same things and that I, too, want to be fully known, even the ugly stuff.

Why do you think Christian leaders predominantly fail under the title "moral failure?" One word: intimacy. In my research, and through personal experience, I have found that the desire to be understood, the desire to connect, the desire to talk to someone who will not judge, and the desire to "be themselves" unfortunately sometimes sinfully outweighs everything else.

To be clear, there is no justification here for sin. It does not exist here. This is a deluded state, many times devoid of worldly and spiritual reality.

People need people, and leaders especially need people. Not only do they need people, but they also hunger to be fully known without fear of repercussion. Sometimes their role seemingly prevents this.

One of the keys to a solid relationship between the board and executive is transparency. An executive has to be able to be transparent, to be themselves. Sometimes that will require their accountability structure to look at them in all of their humanness and move forward with the same compassion, grace, and mercy that they would like to be granted to themselves.

We all have heard that once you find the position that allows you to be yourself completely, it is not work anymore.

This is what everyone wants. This is what every leader wants, and needs.

BE YOURSELF. ALLOWED?

American poet E. E. Cummings wrote in "A Poet's Advice to Students," "To be nobody but yourself—in a world that is doing its best, night and day, to make you everybody else—means to fight the hardest battle which any human being can fight: and never stop fighting." And what is that like as a leader? The fight is magnified under the bright lights.

Being yourself in your role as leader is a commonly held principle, but it is rarely practiced or practical due to fear: fear of not being good enough, fear of looking bad, fear of our deepest self being exposed and not accepted, or fear of lost respect.

Sound familiar?

Some reading this will believe my assertion is wrong and that you are the example of how wrong I am. If it is genuinely true, then congratulations! You are indeed the rare exception.

I recently spent some time with a leader who left from his position at a growing $2 million Christian nonprofit. It was one of those deals where the board gave him a choice: resign or be terminated. In this case, there was no moral failing or money mismanagement, just performance issues. I know because I was on the board that made the difficult decision.

He has since gone on to have a successful consulting business and considers what happened a blessing in disguise.

It was a troublesome time for him and for us as board members. We had meeting after endless meeting praying and discussing what to do, and how to react to the shortcomings of this leader.

We set aside our already busy lives for multiple days in a row for weeks. He went through emotions of self-doubt, measuring his worth as a leader, as a father and husband, and as a man. The work he had put his heart and soul into for several years seemed to all be for naught.

So how could he now look back and see a blessing in disguise? Now he felt like he could be himself again.

When he went to local ballgames, he could just be a father to his children and husband to his wife. He didn't have to scan the crowd to see who was nearby, making sure he acknowledged potential donors or influencers who might impact the organization. If he wanted to get another beer from the concession stand, yell at the umpire, or even just be goofy with his family, no problem.

He could now go to church as himself and not the CEO of the organization. Now he could just go to church, where a big donor to his nonprofit also attended, and not worry about being someone other than himself. If he ran into the donor, okay. If not, no problem. No need any more for hunting them down to make a positive impression. He could now focus on his family without fear that he might say or do the wrong thing.

Another person I interviewed is a fallen executive who ran a $3.5 million rescue mission. This leader fell because of a moral failure and mismanagement of the nonprofit. He said that the stress to fit the mold of a Christian leader, leaving his true self behind, was pressure packed and was a part of his fall and the near destruction of his marriage.

He said he always felt like he had to be careful where he went, where he ate dinner, how he dressed, and with his appearance. Where he attended church was even important.

This former executive feared that he could not show any character flaws—those flaws, he worried, would reflect poorly on the organization and affect donations and support. He told me that he eventually hid out in his condo.

He felt like he had to continually keep up a facade. He always wanted people to think he was superhuman and that he and the organization could accomplish anything. "But you can't let them see you sweat," he said. "If I gave anyone any indication that there was any problem at all, my fear was that they would not contribute or support us in what we were doing."

And this same issue is confirmed to exist in the for-profit business world. Thomas Saporito, CEO of RHR International, points out, "CEOs and other leaders go to great lengths to maintain a facade of unflappable confidence, concealing any insecurities or feelings of anxiety. But this cycle creates dangerous problems for both leaders and their organizations as a whole."[23]

In looking back, concerning the person who was asked to leave the $2 million organization, I think we, as a board, lost confidence in him, and we asked him to leave because he didn't keep a strong enough facade in place. He was battling to not be himself. He is a marvelous person who has proven his value in his field, but possibly was not a suitable fit initially to lead the organization. (Full disclosure—I was also on the same board that hired him in his position.)

Sound familiar? My research indicates most leaders reading this are nodding right about now in agreement and are very familiar with what I have written.

I relate to that sentiment because I lived it.

There were two things my wife would tell you that annoyed her tremendously when I was running a growing nonprofit. First, I could not be myself. I was always trying to impress people. It didn't start that way, but it developed sinfully into this. Some would say this was an individual character flaw, but all leaders struggle with this temptation.

And second, I would never focus on her when we went out. When we went out, I was always looking over her shoulder and scanning the room for potential donors and those that could influence and impact the organization. I also had to always sit facing the entrance so I could watch who entered.

And she was right. Hey, I was building a nonprofit, right? I figured that justified everything. Wrong. Over time, this made her feel devalued, and justifiably so.

LOSING YOUR UNIQUE VOICE

In the book *The Leadership Challenge*, authors James Kouzes and Barry Posner write, "Finding your voice is absolutely critical to becoming an authentic leader." They continue, "If you can't find your voice, you'll end up with a vocabulary that belongs to someone else, mouthing words that were written by some speechwriter, or mimicking the language of some other leader who's nothing like you at all."

Hmm…. A couple questions immediately came to mind: Isn't our natural internal voice something that is lost when we are focused on pleasing people, even if it is in the interest of something good and God honoring? What about the groups that surround the leader, whether or not they are part of their accountability, that continue to pressure the leader to squelch their individual voice in order to please the masses? Did we put them in their position because of their unique creative voice, or because they would succumb? Did we choose them for the right reason? Were they chosen because we thought they would conform?

These are all important questions that need to be asked from now on in whatever role you play in your organization. The pressure to push aside our individual voice creates the rub, the battle within ourselves that can ultimately manifest in discontentment and other issues we discuss in this book.

Without having a true connection to that voice and who they truly are, it doesn't matter how many people are around an executive giving them support and encouragement; they will feel alone, making them susceptible to a fall.

FORGOTTEN IDENTITY

During my time as the president and executive director of our health clinic, my whole life and identity revolved around the organization.

In fact, the wife of one of my friends always had trouble remembering my last name and would refer to me as "Brian (and the name of our organization as my last name)." When I would introduce myself to new people, I would tell them I was the founder of our clinic. Instantly, they would act like they knew me for years.

I fell into the trap of lost personal identity. And eventually my identity in Christ was lost in my pride and arrogance.

In his book *Dangerous Calling*, author Paul David Tripp writes, "I had let ministry become something it should never be (my identity); I looked for it to give me something it never could (my inner sense of well-being)."

One nonprofit CEO I interviewed said, "People identify you as the organization and don't necessarily ask how you are doing. They want to know how the organization is doing."

So, is our identity so wrapped up in the identity of the organization that our judgment of our life depends on the organization's health?

Inappropriately wrapping your identity up in the performance of the nonprofit can be a major problem. When the organization is doing well, we feel confident and ready to conquer the world. When there are stress points in the organization it brings us down, and we question every part of our being, down to a very personal introspective examination.

That roller-coaster ride of instability, no matter which way the pendulum is swinging, can lead to a fall.

Forgetting who we truly are, consciously or unconsciously, in favor of the inaccurate portrait we have painted of ourselves is a temptation to nonprofit leaders, especially executives. Instead of taking a deep look at ourselves, striving for an accurate self-examination, it is easier and less personal to keep our examination and attention on our identity and role as leader of the organization.

On top of that, many times an executive's default view of self comes more in the light of the organization's success or failure and not in light of their own life's walk. When confronted about an issue in their life, in their own mind or by others, they may find themselves responding with statements of what they do in their role, the sacrifices they have made, their accomplishments, the successes they have had, and so on. Many times they become so tied up in that identity and in past successes that they take away their own ability to see an objective accounting of who they currently are.

The new identity may be satisfying as an executive carries out their work, but eventually it catches up with them. When they lay their head on their pillow, or when they truly examine who they are and who they've become, that examination may ring hollow.

An executive has to fight to maintain who they truly are; fight to maintain the identity they had when they came into the executive position. They need to fight to maintain the still, small voice that led them to their current position.

So, what typically comes from continually setting aside who you truly are since you are not good enough? The reality that it is not likely that you will be fully known and still loved? When your unique voice has been squelched or when your true identity has been lost? Loneliness? Isolation? Depression?

LONELINESS AND ISOLATION

I spent most of my adult career managing grocery stores while I also worked in various ministries.

It was not an easy job, and I was sometimes discouraged. Although I knew I was a good store manager, there were always things that made me doubt myself and my performance. I was alone at the top of the store, so I really had no one with whom to discuss my issues. Sure, I could talk to my district manager or call other store managers to talk, but that rarely happened because my pride would not allow it. What would they think of me if they knew I was struggling?

This experience in my life provided me with an excellent case study concerning loneliness and isolation—an experience that would naturally translate into the nonprofit world.

I didn't want the others to think I was anything less than Superman when it came to performing my job. Plus, we all knew there was an underlying competition among us to see who the best was. It didn't matter what the measured parameter may have been: payroll, sales, HR issues, merchandising and supply chain, or health inspections. We wanted to be the best.

I had to keep up the facade of having everything under control, even when I didn't. It had to stay bottled up inside. Pile on top of that the everyday grind of having a target on my back as I tried to balance the needs of the associates with the requirements of the company. It wasn't an easy task and could be very disheartening.

My wife and I found ourselves in a decent spot financially, so we decided to start a business. Recognizing that it would take a few months to iron things out concerning the new business, I gave notice in October that I would be leaving the company during the first week of January. This would allow me to stay during the very busy holiday season.

The company did a wise thing: they removed me from the store I was managing and sent me to stores that needed help during that busy time of year. I would be sort of a co-manager in these stores. What I saw while I worked in these other stores totally changed the way I viewed my job and my performance.

What I saw were the same issues I was having in my own store. The same HR issues: every store had some employees that weren't up to snuff and challenged the management on every point. Every store was struggling to make sales and payroll. Every store struggled to follow the company's merchandising plans and had complaints about supply chain. Every store struggled to impact and articulate the importance of keeping food safety at the top of the agenda. Every store!

The most important thing I saw in nearly every store was how every store manager felt overwhelmed by it all. Every store manager felt like they were on an island. Nearly every store manager felt lonely and felt like they were failing.

I had experienced what they were experiencing, so I related well with them. They were able to bounce things off me in a natural, vulnerable way because I was their equal, but I was leaving. All of this somehow made them feel like they were not alone at the top at that particular time, which was comforting for them.

For me, a tremendous weight was removed from my shoulders as I realized I was not alone; others were dealing with the same challenges. I was not a failure. I was not Superman, but neither was anyone else. Honestly, while I was going through those couple months, I almost decided to stay with the company. I was so relieved, and my confidence was restored.

I have yet to talk to a leader of an organization who does not list loneliness and isolation at the top of their professional challenges.

These are truly the biggest challenges that can lead to a fall.

Many times, this can only be relieved by discussing the experiences of other executives and recognizing you are not truly alone in your struggles. It can be quite comforting.

Starting a nonprofit is hard. Leading it can be just as hard. It is lonely. It can cut you to your very core and make you question who you truly are. I knew that others had to be dealing with the same things I was, and in the same way I was in my previous job.

I started holding regular meetings with three to five nonprofit leaders so we could share and build each other up. I strongly encouraged vulnerability and stripping the facades. This also encouraged unity of the body, as we all worked with an evangelistic mission. We even went so far as to start sitting on each other's boards of directors to encourage that unity. We all agreed that this helped us, and many of those relationships are still strong today.

But what stops us from reaching out to other leaders? Pride? Fear?

Sometimes the struggle of the executive is getting out of their own way.

We need to be true friends with other leaders, beyond the business of running nonprofits. You may be the savior to a fellow leader that is about to fall.

I will be getting deeper into this in Part 3 of the book where I write about a proactive approach, but this is the executive's opportunity to be the leader among leaders.

FRIENDS, REALLY?

In a 2016 research paper involving 8,150 participants for the Schaefer Institute and Churchleadership.org, lead researcher Richard Krejcir wrote that 58 percent of pastors feel they do not have any good, true friends. He also found that 27 percent of pastors have no one to turn to if they are facing a crisis.[24]

One pastor who has served for over 35 years told me that isolation in ministry and not having someone to talk openly and honestly with has been a major problem in his life. "Sometimes when you are struggling as a pastor, people don't necessarily want to know," he said. "They want to know you are real to a certain extent. But when you discuss your struggles, in a lot of cases, they start to lose confidence in you." He explained that sometimes people are not discreet, or they themselves become burdened for you. That's the last thing a pastor wants to be—a burden to their flock.

This same pastor spoke about peer groups that are supposed to help with the pressures of pastoral leadership. He commented that it is even hard for human weakness not to creep into these types of relationships, and that many times people want to talk more about how well they are doing as opposed to sharing their struggles.

Pastors and Christian leaders: how open do you feel in sharing with other leaders, the deep, difficult struggles you experience? We all want to be thought of as successful within our peer groups. This sometimes prevents us from being fully known and limits us to the extent that we are prevented from being spurred on to increased confidence and eventual success.

Most people feel much better when they do an emotional mind dump. Think of how good it feels to have that burden lifted. Most people in their peer groups feel better when they learn others in those same peer groups are dealing with similar things.

Why do you think God told us through the apostle Paul in 1 Corinthians that, "No temptation has seized you except what is common to man?" God knew Paul lived the experience of being out on an island isolated (literally at one point), as if he was the only one with his struggles while carrying out a clear calling from God. He also recognized what a relief it is to humanly see you are not alone.

I do think the pressures weakening a human soul and giving the devil a chance for a foothold need to be acknowledged. It is the responsibility of the leader, as it is with all Christ followers, to guard their hearts and set up boundaries that will keep sin out of their lives.

But I implore you to examine if there is a role that exists for those around believers, especially leaders.

THE PERFECT LEADER

The perfect leader and the perfect organization do not exist.

Every leader wants to do a fabulous job with excellence. They want their organization to be the one that sets the standard. But sometimes this is taken too far.

They want their organization to not just be excellent—they want it to be perfect.

Why? It is because they believe this excellence, this perfection, is a direct reflection on them, and human nature tells them that they want to be well thought of.

Fear of not being perfect, and what it might bring, drives a leader many times. This can be used in a positive way, if managed and properly understood, by inspiring and pushing a leader to a higher level of excellence. It can be used negatively, usually subconsciously, in a way that a leader expects way too much of themselves and those around them.

In fact, on a personal level this sometimes drives a leader to not be themself, as we have already discussed. On a professional level, the drive for perfection by a leader may drive staff, volunteers, and supporters away when they realize they cannot achieve this unrealistic expectation.

Sometimes it is part of a person's makeup, their personal human nature. In the context of this book, it could also be created by the pressure of those around the leader, especially their accountability structure, constituency, or family and friends.

Atelophobia is the fear of imperfection.

In her book *Being Perfect*, Anna Quindlen describes her experience with atelophobia as being "like carrying a backpack full of bricks." She continues, "Oh, how I wanted to lay my burden down."

She discusses how the "illusion of perfection (not being ourselves) requires work that is not portrayed to others." In other words, we want people to think we are just naturally perfect but hide the actions we take to create the illusion. The perfectionist wants to be like the proverbial duck in the water who looks nice and calm as their legs are frantically paddling below the surface.

Quindlen also writes, "If you don't lay your burden down you develop curvature of the spirit." Most of us have seen this "curvature of the spirit" as we have watched leaders become miserable and burn out. They take it upon themselves to keep the organization at a certain level, trying to balance the needs of the organization with personal and family needs.

In a sobering thought for the "perfect leader" that comes from the book, Quindlen states, "Perfection implies a combination of rote and bloodlessness that is essentially made for machines, not men and women."

Perfection is reserved for God and his manifestation in Jesus Christ.

People, you are neither. Leader, you are neither.

We need to stop expecting each other to be.

The desire for, and expectation of, perfection is just one of the many traps an executive can find themselves in.

When a perfection-seeking leader recognizes that it is impossible for them and their organization to be perfect, they become discouraged. Discouragement looks for a pick-me-up, and sometimes that pick-me-up can lead to a fall.

Perfectionists beware.

THE SOMETHING NEW TRAP

Excitement. Vibrancy. Energy. Inspiration. Wonderment. Miraculous.

At the opening of the clinic in early 2013, I witnessed all of these qualities and emotions in abundance. No one could believe that the calling from God came to fruition. From those directly involved to community members, a wave came over everyone. We were all swept up in something much bigger than ourselves.

Everyone was excited to see a fresh way of serving the community taking shape, especially since it was unique and outside the box. To see it all come together and watch God do things that only He could do got people jacked up.

I watched Him do things through me that people thought were impossible, that I thought were impossible. First of all, I had spent a whole career running grocery stores. What did I know about putting together a free health clinic? I had never raised money before or managed a project anywhere near this size. But yet here stood a building fully furnished and adequately staffed after a major renovation project! The stories I could tell.

It was amazing, especially when people dismissed me and said I was crazy.

This stuff gets people wound up. It was my job to keep that energy and excitement going long after we opened and started serving people. The adrenaline rush had to continue for all involved, especially the leadership.

Unfortunately, many leaders find that this is done best by always being able to introduce the next big thing for their organization in order to keep people's attention. That energy becomes addicting.

As a leader, especially as a founder, it's hard to match the satisfaction you experience when you see the excitement in someone's eyes as you share with them a new life-impacting program or piece of equipment that signifies the organization's growth.

Many times the focus becomes more about what the leader is doing instead of what God is doing through them.

It can be a trap if not managed properly with wisdom.

And the people around the leader—staff, supporters, the board, or casual observers—are always asking what's next. They assume there is always something more because of what they have already witnessed. Those around a leader need to be aware of the pressure this creates.

I eventually fell into this trap, an addiction that fuels doing things for appearance and not depth.

While my addiction to the desire to keep people excited about the ministry was motivated by the wrong things, we always performed to the highest level of excellence we were able. Our staff would attest to that. But I have seen it go the other way.

I'm reminded of a large, established organization that serves the homeless, the recovering, and the struggling. They provide counsel, meals, and short-term housing for their clients. They have been the human savior of thousands of men and women who have come through their doorways. Their heart for this demographic is unmatched, and they have been the hands and feet of Christ as they take shattered lives and give hope.

After many years of stale, outdated leadership, the founding leader retired, and a new leader came in.

With any new leader comes an adjustment of the vision and new ways to carry out that vision.

There were some incredible transformations that took place during the first year of this new leadership. The community was excited and refreshed in seeing the change. The organization's new initiatives were reshaping neighborhoods and giving people hope.

The community was excited about the future of the organization, which was reflected in newspapers, news broadcasts, and social media. Big things were happening.

But after a while the momentum slowed. Eventually it got harder and harder for the organization to not only announce new initiatives (the easy part), but also to see them through with excellence (the hard part).

Witnessing the monumental things I was seeing in this organization and having a heart that wanted to see the church grow together through collaboration, I wanted to explore what we might do together.

I met with the leader of the organization, and we came up with the idea of putting an annex of our free clinic in the building where they housed the majority of their clients. It was a win-win, not just for both organizations and their clients, but for the advancement of the Kingdom.

There was no question that this was the direction God wanted us to go. We were already serving a number of their clients at our primary office. We also had a consistent medical provider and staff that were available and could simply report to a different location for work on that particular day.

This was huge! And the community responded with big-time support and encouragement.

At the time, major funders in the area were generally pushing collaboration because they had grown tired of seeing a duplication of services among competing nonprofits.

This project was exactly what they were looking for: two organizations complementing one another, creating synergies, and better serving the community. So funding was not an issue as we quickly secured the grants needed to renovate and get the clinic annex up and running.

The buzz in the community was unbelievable. Everyone was talking about it. We were in the newspaper many times, the TV news was covering us, we sat for interview after interview, and we were doing photo shoots. Really, photo shoots? We even found ourselves on the cover of the local chamber of commerce magazine. It was just a no-brainer, and everyone was pumped.

However, the problem was that while our organization was ready, the other organization was not. Both the other leader and I were in a spot in our ministries that found us constantly searching for the next big thing that would keep our constituencies motivated and excited about the advancement of the organizations in accomplishing our missions. Our infrastructure was strong, so I knew we could take on this new challenge.

But with all the changes already taking place at the other organization, and the resulting internal struggles, they were just not ready. I should have seen it, but again, I was addicted to the look in a person's eye when I told them of the new initiative at the clinic and loved the attention we were getting. So I kept moving forward, even when we were taking on more and more responsibility for the project.

Eventually, it became grueling as we dealt with construction issues in the beginning, then opening issues, scheduling and other procedural issues, and one thing after another. We tried and tried to hold it up from our end the best we could, but it just became nearly impossible.

Finding a workable process was like pulling teeth. It was clear that we missed a stop sign that God had put up in the formation of this project. We had put ourselves and our addictions in front of God's timing in it all.

Eventually, the relationship was ended. Our clinic pulled out because they could not carry the project any further.

I watched this happen a number of times with this organization. They continued to introduce new initiatives that were exceptional and well received in the beginning, but ended up without excellence and eventually flopping.

The expectation of a leader to continually innovate, and the desire the leader has to share the next exciting advancement in an organization is tempting and can be very addicting. Many times, it becomes sinful, and that is always found out.

But many times, this is done with better wisdom, and this ability to innovate is what God uses in a leader to drive an organization forward.

Lesson learned.

TO THE FOUNDERS

A special note to founders that also applies to leaders: don't expect everyone to understand what you are going through and stop trying to "help" those around you understand. Whatever your calling is, assuming it was from God, is between you and God.

The people around you will definitely walk alongside you, encouraging you all along the way. They will do their best to understand what you are going through and will become inspired by what God is doing through you.

But they will not fully understand, and that can be disheartening. I write this so you will not feel alone, like you are crazy. This is normal.

The people on your founding committee or board will not understand. The community will not understand. Collaborators will not understand. Funders will not understand, and almost certainly, your spouse will not understand.

The more you try to help them understand, the more they will be driven away and alienated. Then the loneliness and isolation follows.

I can assure you they are giving you their best.

Stop it! God is the only one who gets it because He gave you the calling.

I realized, as a founder, when I went to other organizational executives for support and compassion that they just didn't get it either. Now that's not to say that hired executives are not super valuable, don't have huge hearts for the work of God and the ministry, and don't sacrifice greatly for the mission, but it is quite different. I quickly realized that the only people who got it were other founders.

I found guidance and mentorship from other founders.

One of my mentors founded a private school in 1998, and two decades later the school has a budget over $3 million and serves 250 mainly urban youth. She understood what I was going through.

Many times I thought I was completely losing it and she was able to give me some story from her past that delivered comfort and understanding at the right time. Through her personal stories, she helped me to escape from isolation and to develop the feeling that I was not alone, that I was not nuts, and that God's got this. Each time she shared insight with me a portion of the burden was lifted from my shoulders.

She continued to share stories in her journey of founding the school, but it wasn't until the clinic was opened and running that she told me the rest of the story. I found it to be a universal one that I've heard from other founders over the years. In her words:

> There were many circumstances that contributed to my "breakdown." A thousand little things not going as I'd anticipated, people expressing their dissatisfaction with this and that, too much negative self-talk. I felt overwhelmed and alone. At the time, I felt responsible for the investment of every stakeholder, employee, donor,

student, parent, and board member. Whether or not it was true, I perceived that as the founder and leader, the success or failure of the organization rested solely on me. The culmination of circumstances, my thoughts, and my emotions manifested in such anxiety and immobility that I required medical and spiritual/emotional attention. Looking back, I'd say that unrealistic expectations of myself as well as ego played a role, but foremost was the lack of wisdom in forming a supportive infrastructure to assist in practical ways in addition to providing perspective.

I related to every single word. I was taking on way too much of the responsibility myself instead of leaning on God. He was the one that threw out the call (remember, our responsibility is to listen and be faithful and the rest is on Him).

Founders, your calling introduces you to the ultimate challenges in leadership. Your journey is arduous. I sit in awe of you and empathize with your plight.

But you are called. That is the key and needs to be your main focus and source of comfort.

Would I have fallen had I not been afraid to be fully known, had I been able to be myself without repercussion, had I had friends that would have allowed me to be fully vulnerable and transparent, had the people around me paid attention? Would I have fallen if my true self had not been squelched in favor of conformity and acceptance, and had I not been tempted toward some of the traps of leadership? Would I have fallen?

I will never know because I made the wrong choices out of my humanness.

But one thing I know is this: the desire to be fully known, to have people you can count on, and to be yourself lie at the intersection of a leader being fully human, with all of their frailties and imperfections, and being a solid, long-term leader of an organization. Without a full acknowledgment and examination of this within an organization, the organization leaves itself vulnerable to a leadership fall.

CHAPTER 5

THE BOARD OF DIRECTORS CHALLENGE

NONFUNCTIONING. Dysfunctional. Unengaged. Nepotistic. Those words describe the first board I served on almost 30 years ago. This food bank board was run by the founder who had been there for decades. The chairman of the board was a fantastic individual who happened to be a pastor.

The board members, including me, consisted of people who were mainly brought on the board through the founder. At the time I was early in my career managing grocery stores, which naturally tied in with the food bank's purpose. These were good people with good hearts.

The board meetings were conducted in a way that you would expect considering the adjectives listed above. We would arrive at the meeting place and shoot the breeze as we waited to see how many of the members were going to show up, which meant we rarely started on time. The chairman would keep a count to see if we had a quorum in order to vote on action items. That voting usually consisted of approving the previous meeting's minutes and the financial reports. Most months when we did have a quorum we would vote on multiple items from previous months when we didn't have one.

The board was on autopilot. It was too easy because the founder seemed to run everything so smoothly.

The executive director/founder was trusted and worked with very little accountability. When challenged with a question he became defensive, so no one asked difficult questions.

The bylaws were as outdated as the organization itself.

The assistant executive director was the son of the executive director/founder. He was in line to take over when his father retired, which turned out to be within two years.

I entered this situation with an idealistic view of all of the great things this board was going to do. I was enthusiastic and ready to get to work. But I was young and naive.

There was no orientation, so the acronyms and operational terminology that were thrown around were confusing, and I couldn't keep up. I had no idea what my role was or what the expectations of me were, other than to show up. Eventually it was announced that the founder would be retiring and he would like his son to take over as the leader of the organization, which the board rubber-stamped.

The drama that ensued during the transition revealed financial and operational malfeasance. After a very strong effort to fix the issues, much of the board, including me, resigned.

It was ugly. Support for the organization suffered so much so that I heard the organization nearly had to fold.

I am glad to say that the organization did not fold and has a very distinguished and responsible board of directors at this time. It has been a complete 180-degree turnaround.

Since then, I have served on numerous boards and have never had an experience like that again. My board experiences for the most part have been positive. Not perfect, but mostly productive and life-impacting for me and the clients served.

But I'll bet elements of my story do seem familiar to experienced board members and leaders. My story highlights some of the things that happen on boards, many times leading to major trouble for the organization.

It is this type of culture on a board of directors that causes them to forget why they are there and why they originally joined. It is this type of culture on a board that causes them to stop paying attention to the important things. It is this type of culture on a board that causes them to miss the warning signs that a leader may be falling. It is this type of culture that causes a board to look at each other in surprise as they are forced to deal with the ramifications and collateral damage of a leadership fall.

This chapter is written to acknowledge the difficult and frustrating parts of being on a board that bog the directors down and draw their attention away from those things that can make or break an organization, including a leadership fall.

THE INDIVIDUAL BOARD MEMBER

The individual board member must be wise, but humble. They must be an independent thinker, but able to compromise. They must be objective, but focused. An individual board member must be informed, but teachable. They must be bold in expression, but eager to listen. They must be passionately engaged, but not overbearing.

It's not easy. The list of board member attributes above is all about balance—appropriate balance.

But, as is one of the main principles of this book, board members are human. It is nearly impossible to hit all of the marks included in the above attributes. They form an ideal devoid of fallible human nature.

There are two attributes not listed above that rise to the top and are much more important than any others. Two attributes that should be present in the life of a board member that are vital in directing an organization, especially in adversity, are integrity and courage.

Integrity. A common definition of integrity, relating to the character of people, would say that integrity is the quality of being honest and having strong moral principles. Another definition, related to tangible items, would be that the item is sound, unimpaired, and of flawless condition.

Considering the combination of those two common definitions of integrity reminds me of a lesson that was taught by Pastor Dan Branda in my home church Sunday school at least 10 years ago.

He taught that one feature of integrity was about making every effort to stay true to who you have publicly expressed you are in Christ in every facet of life, whether that be in public or private. I would add that the integrity he taught in a Christian context could be applied to any commitment we make in life, especially those involving our character.

Integrity in the context of this book, and specifically in the context of this chapter, means doing your absolute best as a board member to hold up to those original commitments you made when you joined the board. If the board of directors you joined happens to be that of a Christian nonprofit, then maintaining integrity as a Christian needs to be part of the equation.

Courage. Most common definitions of courage have something to do with overcoming fear. Merriam-Webster says courage is the mental or moral strength to venture, persevere, and withstand danger, fear, or difficulty.

A board member must have the courage to stand alone, even in the face of friends, family, and those closest to them. They must be listeners and must be able to evaluate what they hear in the proper context of whatever the situation may be, but they must also have the courage to challenge and stand alone if need be. Yes, sometimes this comes with risk and fear: fear of what others will think of them, fear of lost respect, fear of judgment, and fear that they may simply be wrong. This is where courage comes in.

This means a board member must be able to stand up for what they believe in and ask difficult questions when needed despite the perceived consequences. This is integrity and courage in a board of director's context.

For the individual board member, sprinkling integrity and courage over all of the attributes mentioned at the beginning of this section and balancing them as you work with a team to provide direction for their nonprofit is an absolute must. When these attributes come naturally and are part of the board member's character, well, they are the perfect board member.

But no one is perfect, and this forms an inherent problem, especially in adversity.

This book does not ask for perfection. But it does encourage the extension of grace and mercy to humans who are flawed, especially leaders. So please, do not take it personally, but evaluate what might apply to you.

Again, it's not easy. All board members go through times of difficulty when they question what benefit they are to the board and organization, or times when their integrity and courage are weakened, often as the result of dysfunction on the board.

Questioning yourself during times that require courage is normal. This is why solid, encouraging board relationships are important, and why those relationships must be nurtured as part of the structure of the board.

Although I am writing to encourage the increased relationship between the board and executive, the board's awareness of one another as fallible, imperfect human beings is also very important in the success of an organization.

Let's take this a little further and look at the board of directors as a team—a group of individual board members coming together to work toward the common goal of organizational success.

THE BOARD AS A TEAM

A board of directors must have integrity and courage. The team must be wise but humble. They must be independent thinkers, but able to compromise. They must be objective, but focused. A board of directors must be informed, but teachable. They must be bold in expression, but eager to listen. They must be passionately engaged, but not overbearing.

Yes, the collective board of directors has the same attributes as the individual board member. But, as a body, they have the added fiduciary responsibility of directing the organization, with consideration of the pressure from the community, to act in a way that is expected of their organization.

I started with the individual board member for this very reason. The board is made up of individuals, albeit imperfect individuals, that bring their individual character traits to the board, thereby forming a body with those same traits and attributes.

All of this to say that the board is not perfect, and we should not expect anything else. While it is wise to understand that imperfection is inherent in a board of directors, that weakness does form a problem.

This problem, while part of the human condition, sometimes makes it difficult for a board to operate as a cohesive team with the enthusiasm, wisdom, and drive that is required to make an organization successful.

This difficulty sometimes ultimately causes a board to focus on its own operation and survival in a way that takes for granted its relationship with the executive and staff.

In other words, they stop paying attention to those running the organization to a level that could be detrimental to its success.

Just like nearly any group of people, whether it be a team, a class, a work group, or even in the marketplace, boards struggle with how they see themselves as a group and how they see each other as individual board members. There are many parts of human nature, as discussed previously, that enter into the equation when it comes to relating to each other and the executive leadership of the organization.

Problems that occur in a boardroom are often simply human nature issues. Instead of me listing all of the correlations between human nature and the problems in a boardroom, let's take a look at some statistics using board members as the providers of the data.

The Stanford Graduate School of Business in collaboration with BoardSource and Guidestar surveyed 924 directors of nonprofit organizations about the composition, structure, and practices of their boards. Their study found that:

- 27% of nonprofit directors do not believe their fellow board members have a strong understanding of the mission and strategy of their organization,

- 32% are not satisfied with the board's ability to evaluate the performance of the organization,

- 65% of those surveyed do not believe the directors on their board are very experienced,

- 48% do not believe their fellow directors are very engaged in their work,

- 47% of nonprofit directors believe that their fellow board members understand their obligations as directors well, and

- 69% of nonprofit directors say their organization has faced one or more serious,governance-related problems in the past 10 years.[25]

So, what do you see? Clearly the opinions of the board member respondents to this survey reveal that nonprofit boards have work to do in their own development. They themselves believe they are unqualified, uninformed, and don't understand their board obligation.

The first thing I questioned as I read the complete report was how these 924 directors personally rated themselves as individual board members. Unfortunately, this was not included in this excellent report. When answering questions like this for a survey, I believe it is only human nature that the respondents are measuring the skills and attributes of fellow board members against their impression of their own performance on the board.

And round and round we go. Human nature again.

Boards have their own issues, whether they be recruitment and onboarding issues, training issues, leadership issues, ego issues, human nature issues, expertise issues, relationship issues, governance issues, or any number of other issues.

Please recognize that this is not a book about how to create properly functioning boards. If needed, I strongly recommend board training from a qualified local organization or consultant that can be brutally honest, yet effectively encouraging in the changes needed to function better. I had to do this very thing while leading our organization as executive and doubling as chairman of the board at its founding.

The people around an executive leader can be proactive in the prevention of a fall. The accountability structure, or board of directors, is a big part of that. But they must stay focused.

It's extremely important to recognize that a board that is not functioning properly, and not consciously evaluating their own performance will have great difficulty in being a proactive force in the evaluation and guidance of an executive.

FROM THE START

According to BoardSource, "Nothing is more important to the health and sustainability of your organization than getting highly qualified and enthusiastic people to serve on your board. But many organizations struggle to identify the right leaders."[26]

Oh, how true that is. Keeping the board vibrant and fresh is one of the biggest challenges of a nonprofit organization. Some do it well, but most struggle.

BoardSource also reports that 58 percent of nonprofit leaders find it difficult to recruit new board members.

Every leader wants great talent on their board that just happens to have a high level of experience and a vast network for raising funds.

I have served on boards that are very purposeful when considering potential new members they would like to recruit. And it shows. But I have also served on boards that find themselves trying to fill slots on the board at all cost. And it shows.

Sure, they have standards, but those standards fluctuate depending on the need. I have watched boards bend standards that were developed based on their core principles in the recruiting of new board members, principles that make them who they are. When standards are bent, we like to think that the potential board member doesn't see it, but they do.

This can start a cycle in their personal board membership that bends standards and makes them a sloppy member of the team as standards and expectations come across as flexible.

This especially happens when organizational leaders want to build credibility for their organization. This causes them to desire to have big names on their board or to have certain categories of directors serving.

For instance, a Christian social service agency would want a pastor and members of the community they are serving on their board. That makes sense, but to what extent are they willing to bend to fill the categories as they build that credibility?

It's hard not to be sympathetic to the plight of leadership struggling to recruit the exact people they need on their board. I know I continually had a difficult time and bent the standards myself. And it showed.

To the top-notch board member or board chair, it can be very frustrating working to build a board of qualified members. As we've seen, it is a common problem. When the focus of the board and its leadership is taken away by tasks such as recruitment of board members, it is even more difficult for them to pay attention to the subtle cues of a leader falling. But board recruitment is a necessary evil.

Even if the board leadership finds itself with some decent new recruits, are they being onboarded properly?

Green, Hasson & Janks is a Los Angeles-based accounting and tax consulting firm that takes nonprofits seriously as they work to provide value to that nonprofit community. In 2018 they published a whitepaper report that had some interesting statistics concerning onboarding of new board members. The survey revealed the following:

- 12% of respondents said new board members attend mandatory board training,
- 16% have a formal onboarding process or are developing one, 35% of respondents said new members are provided with an information packet prior to their first meeting,
- 42% of board members fully understand their organization's programs, and

- 58% of board chairs set clear expectations for board members.[27]

The numbers speak for themselves, and any veteran board member has to agree that they have experienced this very thing. Proper onboarding of new board members seriously lacks and causes major lapses in focus as those new members are receiving their on-the-job training.

Improper recruitment and onboarding of potential and new board members causes most of the struggles on boards. These two things have to be done right. Without them being given the proper attention they need, the board will run circles around themselves and be unproductive. This lack of productivity and frustration will cause the board to be preoccupied with its own operation, with the needs of the organization and support of its leadership becoming secondary.

In other words, the board will be paying attention to the wrong things.

The proper choosing and vetting of potential board members, along with proper orientation of those board members, is vital. Without these two things at the genesis of board membership, they could be left confused, frustrated, and to their own devices. This can cause commitment to vary, and may cause motivation to be lost. With that, board mediocrity and organizational difficulty may be on the horizon.

VARYING LEVELS OF COMMITMENT

Every board member looks at their commitment to the organization differently. During the interview and vetting of a potential new board member, the desired level of commitment concerning time, talent, and treasure are discussed. The organization must clearly lay out accurate expectations concerning these three things so the candidate can make a good decision and both can assure a good fit on the board.

Just as human nature would dictate, the board wants all they can get out of the new board member, and the board member has their limitations.

Hopefully, both of these can be worked out, and it is a good fit.

But sometimes there is not a good fit, and the person ends up on the board anyway for some of the reasons previously described. This can create board dysfunction and drama that pulls the attention of the board away from those things that truly need it.

And a board is no different than all of society, encompassing a diverse work ethic from those that go overboard to those that struggle to meet the minimums. This is why a clear expectation needs to be discussed at the beginning of board service.

Different boards require different expectations based on the type of organization, its size, and perhaps the age of the organization.

For instance, when I formed the first board for our health clinic, the board positions were functional, and the board, in many cases, worked as staff. I really needed them, and the board filled the roles of human resources, accounting, business management, community engagement, and spiritual guidance.

If I'm being honest, the commitment expectations I had for each of our board members were not clearly laid out, and this caused some issues. It was my fault entirely.

The varying levels of commitment of board members can cause friction between individual board members and between the board and paid staff.

Again, this struggle can cause a board to lose focus on the things that are important such as operational deficiencies, financial management, and the monitoring of the executive.

WHERE ARE THE LINES?

"The lines" are those unwritten places where a leader's (board member or executive) words and actions can become inappropriate or unproductive.

Examples of the lines that may get crossed might be the length of meetings, when the discussion of a topic gets cut off, what topics are taboo and don't get discussed, amount of operational guidance, level of commitment of board members, or any number of elephant-in-the-room topics. Needless to say, the crossing of some imaginary lines can cause friction within a board of directors.

And the big line that becomes the elephant in the room: how deep do we dig into an executive's personal life? Yes, the executive does a nice job pulling together all of the reports and presenting them to the board in a clear, concise, and articulate manner. They seem to be well-liked by the board, the staff, and the community.

But you start to sense something is wrong, and you start to catch some verbal cues from the executive. You start to hear rumblings about some issues in their personal life. They seem to be doing a really good job technically, but you fear they may be struggling inside.

Is this even a board issue? Where is the line? If you step over that line and you are wrong, it may hurt the organization, you may look bad, or you will get harshly judged yourself.

Each board has their lines based on the history of the organization, the style of the leadership, and the personalities of the board members.

So, where are the lines in an organization?

Of course, there is no singular answer to this question. People are people, and the lines are ever changing. Those lines can change based on a conversation a board member had just before the meeting, the mood they are in, or who is attending a particular meeting. Sometimes it is just that random.

It doesn't matter how long someone has served on a particular board, they are still figuring out, and massaging, where those lines are.

Figuring out where the lines are, and abiding by them, can be the difference between a harmonious board and one that is divided. Even more importantly, and I would say more productively, is knowing how far a line can be crossed.

Lines need to be crossed, but doing so in a positive way that communicates interest in the advancement of the organization is absolutely the key.

Without productively crossing lines an organization cannot grow and advance in their field, therefore impacting more people. Leaders must have courage in order to cross the lines and challenge the status quo for the betterment of the organization. For example, sometimes a board is financially conservative, almost to a fault. The suggestion of drawing down reserves in order to invest in a new program is a line no one likes to cross. Board members give a fellow board member "the look" when the topic is broached. But perhaps having the courage to cross that line may bring a greater impact to a community and actually increase the organization's financial security through increased exposure.

But this can be a struggle, dividing the board and creating cliques and factions around a particular idea.

It takes a mature, experienced, and skilled board chair to navigate these waters while guiding the board in maintaining the already important work that is being accomplished. This maintenance includes the watchful eye they must have in monitoring the leadership of the organization.

Crossing unwritten and imaginary lines, and the drama that can ensue, is just another practical area that can draw the attention of the board from those things that are most important in directing an organization.

WHO DID WE FORGET?

The board of directors always has as their chief desire the advancement of the organization. This advancement can be defined many ways, all around the central mission of the organization.

Some may define advancement, or success, of the organization in financial terms. Some may measure it in terms of missional impact. Some may define advancement in terms of increased organizational stability.

An issue I have seen crop up is that the zeal of the board for organizational success, no matter how it is defined, sometimes causes them to take the paid leadership and staff for granted, which can cause friction and a break in the relationships.

This is not something any board member wants to happen, but sometimes it happens in the course of doing business and putting out fires. The problem is that many times it is only recognized after catastrophe.

About 10 years ago, I sat on the board of a health education center that caters mainly to schoolchildren. They were, and still are, having a huge impact. This was a large board made up of a who's who list among local businesspeople and organizational leaders.

Just like many businesses and nonprofits have experienced, the model had increasingly changed over time. The years of the school busses pulling up to the front door and dropping off hundreds of children to experience the best in health education had changed. This was still happening on a limited basis, but the operation of the mission had largely yielded to the educators going out to the schools and to online and electronically recorded technology.

The organization was great at positioning itself in the community in order to raise money and increase their impact. Many years ago the organization realized that the key to increased growth and sustainability could be found by expanding their geographical reach.

The focus became looking outside the local community, and with advancements in technology it really made sense. At the time I had a concern that this focus was becoming too strong and that we were forgetting about our own backyard, even taking it for granted. I thought that we should be doing more grassroots-type work in our neighborhoods to impact those directly around us.

The center sits in the middle of an urban community that struggles with poverty and many of the social ills we see in our country.

Of course, with those social ills come many opportunities concerning health education. I felt we had a higher responsibility to the neighborhood we were in and could take advantage of our unique positioning to move the needle in our home community.

During my time addressing the full board I drew this analogy: I felt like we, as a board, were standing on the top of our roof by the edge, looking out over the vast world in front of us. We were looking at the far reaches of states far away, envisioning what impact our organization could have way out there, as well as the mission-oriented support that could be gained by being there. We would then turn our heads or move to the edge of the building on the other side and see the same thing with even more opportunity.

What we lacked on that trip to the roof as we looked out far and wide to see the opportunities of other states and communities was the ability to look straight down to where we physically were. We were possibly missing opportunities in our own community. My goal was to take us back to a time when the local community was the main focus, the only focus. My goal was to pump the breaks and see if we were doing all we could in our immediate neighborhood while still looking for opportunities in the far reaches.

I believe that many organizations do this to our leaders. We, as a board, stand on the roof in one corner by the edge seeing the great expanse with all of the great things we have done, the incredible advances we have made, and the lives we have helped change. If you are a Christian organization, you see all of the blessings and support you have received from God in making it all happen. You tear up as you consider what He has done and how He has used you in that effort.

We, as a board, move to another corner and look far out there to see all of the opportunities of the future and the advancements that need to be made, the broken lives that need to change, and the people searching for answers that we might just have.

We consider the money that needs to be raised, but after considering what God has already done, we are confident He will continue to bless. It's quite humbling.

But we sometimes fail to look straight down to see our leadership (and sometimes staff) barely hanging on, taken for granted as if the accomplishment of a job description is a foregone conclusion and automatic. As we reflect on accomplishments of the past and dream of the incredible future God has for us as an organization, we sometimes forget that as we drive forward there are real people involved. Too often we look past them, barely seeing them and their struggles.

Just like standing on the roof at the health education center, our leaders are our neighborhood, and they need to be taken care of first if we are going to perform our missions with excellence.

BUT SOMETIMES THE EXECUTIVE...

I've been pretty hard on the board and the individuals who serve on a board. I get it. Even as I wrote some of what I did previously in this chapter, I found myself pondering thoughts that started with, "But sometimes the executive...." Maybe you did too.

Sometimes the executive, and the personal and professional characteristics that made them the executive, contribute to the issues on a board.

It happened in my experience on the food bank's board.

While the executive director was a solid Christian man with a wonderful heart toward those with food insecurity issues, he contributed to the dysfunction on the board.

As the founder, he thought he had all of the answers, and when challenged, he became defensive. He wanted to recruit new board members, but for the most part, he did not ensure proper training of those board members. He pushed his son to be the new executive and worked to manipulate the board into the rubber-stamping of him as his replacement, qualified or not. Of course, the board should have had more courage in the fight, but the executive made it a fight. No one likes a fight.

So, all issues are not necessarily the fault of the board itself. There are two main members of the leadership team of an organization, the board and the executive, and both members must be respectful of the other. If not, the board is forced to take the upper hand as they legally are obligated to do. We didn't do it on that food bank board.

Sometimes it is the executive who creates division on the board as they meet separately with board members working to garner support for their position concerning a controversial topic. While doing this, factions or cliques can be created that cause dysfunction.

A strong-willed executive can also be a difficult force to reckon with on a nonprofit board. Sometimes the executive doesn't understand their role as it relates to the board and actually tries to run the board.

And then you have the executive who constantly complains about wanting more engagement from the board. But ultimately, do they? I have found that this is sometimes legitimate and sometimes it is not.

One former executive I interviewed was always complaining about the noninvolvement of the board in their organization. He said, "There was no interaction, and they didn't care what I did as long as the numbers were right."

The board eventually did get involved as he recruited members with a higher level of expertise and board governance experience. As the new members became more involved, he complained that, "They kind of turned on me." He said, "I wanted to move forward, and they wanted to slow me down."

So, I surmised that this executive really didn't want more engagement from the board but wanted to blame his own shortcomings on them. Yes, sometimes the executive is the issue and makes it difficult to focus on the business of the board.

———————————

As with leadership in general, nonprofit board leadership can be a tremendously rewarding experience that brings out the best in a person and the joys of life. Most people beam with pride as they talk about their experiences as a board member and all that is being accomplished in the organization they serve.

But that's not always the case. Boards are made up of people. The inherent problems that fallible, imperfect people can bring to a board can shift their correct focus away from those things that are most important to the organization.

Many times the board is confident in the executive leadership of the organization and takes them for granted as their focus is shifted to the more immediate needs of the board, sometimes simple board dysfunction. Just like nonprofit executive leadership, board leadership is hard. It can be very frustrating.

I have never served on the perfect board. There are always challenges and difficulties in balancing all of the priorities of the organization and the individuals serving on the board. I think of the performer spinning plates on stage who is always going to the plate that is ready to smash to the floor.

Once they get that one spinning strong, there is always another one ready to fall.

Each time a board seemed to be running well, and I thought I was on the perfect board, a difficulty would force me out of that type of thinking. But that's also one thing I like about boards: they're always changing and always challenging.

PART 3

THE PROACTIVE
APPROACH

THE NEXT THREE chapters are about action. Action based on the recognition of the other perspectives you gained in Part 2.

Through a tough examination of yourself and the organization you are involved with, you have recognized that it is entirely possible that a fall could happen in your nonprofit. You previously may have seen cracks, but did not realize what those cracks could turn into.

You may now recognize that the indicators you have been seeing and thinking about are real, needing to be talked about before there is a disaster.

The problems that lead to a nonprofit leadership fall have now been defined. You are able to relate to one of the roles I used in the previous chapters and have also gained a new perspective on those that you are familiar with but do not live in. You recognize that simple human nature has its own role.

Assumptions have been pushed aside, and you maybe have come out of Part 2 even more curious about other roles in a nonprofit organization.

You've really been touched and recognize that the love of your organization must force you to look at things from a different reality, one that must manifest in action. Without action your organization could be damaged or at least be placed in peril.

Executive, it's time to examine yourself, Courageously Ask difficult questions, and build walls and hedges of protection where they need to be built. Accountability structure, it's not good enough to care about your executive; you must make sure they know it, and it is part of your management. And, community, it's time to reach out and support.

All, it's time to make decisions.

No longer are you able to expect someone else to take care of what you have been watching or have been concerned about.

Now it's time to really take this thing seriously. But where do you go from here?

CHAPTER 6

LEADER, IT STARTS WITH YOU

MANY LEADERS, ESPECIALLY executives, are bottom-line people. It doesn't matter if they are working to urgently solve a problem, analyzing a financial report, or listening to a waitress describe the ins and outs of the BLT they are ordering, they want the bottom line.

Executives have different styles to get to the bottom line, and they are wide ranging. Some are gently and artfully persuasive in guiding a conversation to the bottom line, and some are very direct, almost insulting.

This is one of those places in the book where I will be very direct, get to the bottom line, maybe step on your toes in challenging your thinking.

I absolutely, whole-heartedly believe that those who surround a leader play a significant role in preventing their fall, especially when they see them falling.

But, I do wish to include one harsh caveat to that fact. One bottom-line, very biblical principle directed at the executive: **you are ultimately accountable.**

For those around the executive leader who have been waiting for me to say it, there it is. The leader is accountable for their own life and the decisions they make.

For all of modern society this can be a truth that is difficult to face. It's a truth that many want to sweep under the rug as we live in a "do-what-you-think-is-right, what-makes-you-feel-good" society. Just because it is common does not make it true or acceptable.

There are many things that an executive leader can do to be proactive in their fight against a fall.

The very first thing they need to do after acknowledging they are accountable for their continued thoughts, words, and actions is to enter the fight. They have to realize they are in a multifaceted battle and recognize that, against all apparent odds, they could succumb to one of the many temptations that could bring them and their organization down.

If you, as a leader, don't think this is possible, you may want to go back and read Chapter 1. It is possible. In fact, without conscious effort, it is probable.

This chapter is written to help you as a leader strategize your unique battle plan, so you will not only win the battle, but also be a conqueror in your own personal war that goes beyond nonprofit leadership.

IT COMES BACK TO ME?

"If your health fails, your marriage hits the rocks, or your finances reverse, people will feel sorry for you, but they won't feel responsible. Why not? Because you're the one who has to take responsibility for your own life." *Ouch!* Those are the words of Patrick Morley in his book *Ten Secrets for the Man in the Mirror.*

James Allen puts it this way in his 1903 book, *As a Man Thinketh*: "A man's weakness and strength, purity and impurity, are his own, and not another man's; they are brought about by himself, never by another. His condition is also his own, and not the other man's. His suffering and his happiness are evolved from within. As he thinks, so he is."

When I think about individual accountability, Ezekiel 18:20 always come to mind: "The soul who sins is the one who dies."

Sounds like Patrick Morley and James Allen were simply stating what God said through the prophet Ezekiel way back around 570 BC. You see, the Israelites kept repeating a proverb that they felt allowed them to blame their ancestors for the path they chose for their own lives. Ezekiel received a word from the Lord that took out that trap door of escape. In fact, he says it more than once in just this one chapter of the book and explains it thoroughly. We can find individual accountability all throughout God's word, but this one always sticks out most to me.

It's a hard thing to face, but when we have to account for our lives on judgment day, we will not be able to blame anyone else for how we ran our lives.

This book talks a lot about the grace and mercy that needs to be applied to the encouragement and treatment of a leader, but a leader has to be cautious that their humanness does not become an excuse for sin.

Before all of this reality settles too far deep inside of you and you panic, God also gives us tremendous support, hope, and encouragement in that reality. For instance, in 2 Peter He tells us that He has given us everything we need for life and godliness through our knowledge of Him who called us. And what about 1 Corinthians 10 where He tells us through Paul that He is faithful and will not let us be tempted beyond what we can bear and will provide a way out so that we can stand up under it? These are promises of God. And if God promises it, you can take it to the bank.

The wise Christian will ask God for help and will always find that, even though they are hanging on by just one nail and the enemy is trying to pry that nail loose, God will open a window of hope and allow you into safety. Many times the window appears in your life in the form of God's promises.

So we, including nonprofit executives, are accountable for our own lives. In today's world, that can be depressing and shoot us into despair. But God's promises, if we choose to avail ourselves of them, provide hope and encouragement even during the toughest of times.

TINY CRACKS?

A fall starts small—taking some office supplies home, putting your lunch on the expense account, a glance, an extended look, a temporary fantasy, daydreaming, cutting out an hour early, or clicking an ad on the Internet. These are all seemingly small things in and of themselves, but can also be sinful in their own right and context. Absent of healthy accountability, self-judgment, and evaluation, any one of these can trigger a downward spiral to disaster in the life of a nonprofit executive.

Each individual has different triggers. Perhaps none of these, or maybe one of many others, could trigger a disaster in your life. Maybe your trigger is something totally different. One thing I am absolutely certain of is that the enemy knows which one will get it started, no matter how small. And his game is long.

All of this writing about small things that can turn into a disaster reminds me of the tiny crack that can turn into an avalanche. That might seem like a big jump, but allow me to explain.

Beginning skiers start out usually by teaming up with someone who knows how to ski or is skilled in teaching the sport.

Typically they start with the bunny hill, and usually over a number of years gain the confidence and skill to make it to the top of the mountain.

Their skill level has taken them to a place where they themselves are able to teach rookies the skills that will help them achieve their goals on the slopes.

Sound familiar at all? To me, the development of a skilled, top-notch skier follows a similar path as the development of a successful Christian leader. Read back over the previous paragraph with that perspective. Hmm...

For some skiers that go on to conquer the most challenging slopes at ski resorts across the world, they find themselves bored, even on the black diamond slopes, and move onto uncharted mountains without the ski patrol to fall back on. This allows them to recapture the adrenaline rush they once had as they honed their skills and overcame challenges to get to their current level.

Are you following with the Christian leader in mind?

According to Avalanche.org, nearly all avalanche deaths in North America are something called "dry slab avalanches." They go on to explain, "If you're looking for the killer, the slab avalanche is your man. This is the White Death, the Snowy Torrent, the Big Guy in the White Suit." (Does this sound like the description of a nonprofit executive fall?)

A "slab" is a cohesive plate of snow that slides as a unit on the snow underneath. Picture tipping the living room table up on edge and a magazine slides off the table. Now picture yourself standing in the middle of the magazine. The crack forms up above you, and there you are; there's usually no escape, and you're off for the ride of your life.

To those Christian nonprofit leaders who have fallen, this will sound familiar.

The bonds holding a slab in place typically fracture at about 220 miles per hour, and it appears to shatter like a pane of glass. It's typically about the size of half a football field, usually about one to three feet deep, and typically reaches speeds of 20 miles per hour within the first three seconds and quickly accelerates to around 80 miles per hour after the first, say, six seconds.

Now, catch this, also from Avalanche.org:

> *Dry slab avalanches can lie patiently, teetering on the verge of catastrophe, sometimes for days to even months. The weak layers beneath slabs are also extremely sensitive to the rate at which they are stressed. In other words, the rapid addition of the weight of a person can easily initiate the fracture on a slope that would not have avalanched otherwise. A slope can lay in waiting like a giant booby trap—just waiting for the right person to come along. The crack often forms well above the victim leaving little room for escape. Does any of this sound dangerous to you?*

Personally, I have experienced this metaphorical avalanche in my own life.

One more fact: the general consensus seems to be that the speed of Olympic downhill skiers tends to fall in the 80 miles per hour range, with some exceeding even 90 miles per hour on the fastest sections of the course. Recreational downhill skiers often average a speed somewhere between 20 to 40 miles per hour.[28]

Can a skier outrun an avalanche? It seems that the likelihood is better that the same skier might be able to win the lottery. It's exactly the same when a catalyst triggers a leadership fall.

Do you see the parallels between the fall of a onetime solid Christian leader and the fatality of a solid skier in an avalanche? I will limit my observations to just 10:

1. Preparation: Both spend a lot of time in preparation, starting with no knowledge or skill, having to learn from the ground up.

2. Focus: Both focus intently on the skill, many times making it their highest priority.

3. Training: Both pull people more experienced than themselves into their world in order to learn the skills needed. Many become the trainer.

4. Development: Both spend many years honing their skill, continually reaching for the next level.

5. Drive: Both have a drive that many people do not understand.

6. Control (always an illusion): Both have difficulty regaining control after the disaster has started.

7. Confidence: Both can get to a level where they feel invincible.

8. Disaster potential: Both have a disaster potentially waiting just below the surface for that one relatively small catalyst to start the disaster.

9. Escape: Both can escape a catastrophe, but it is extremely rare once the small catalyst has been activated.

10. Collateral Damage: Huge for both.

Executive, are you paying attention?

Without proper identification and acknowledgment of catalysts that can activate potential disasters currently lying just below the surface, the likelihood of a disaster, a leadership fall, happening is greatly increased.

Take note that there are two factors I mentioned above that are needed to facilitate a disastrous fall in the life of a nonprofit executive leader, as well as a skier:

1. A potential disaster below the surface, and

2. A catalyst to activate that potential.

I submit to you that most executives, in the deepest part of who they are, can identify potential temptations in their particular life that can lead to a disastrous fall. As is human nature, they think they have it under control.

Little do they know that there is a catalyst that just might come along to activate that disastrous temptation and take it beyond their control. I know this because it is what happened in my world.

It's time to commit to a proactive approach in avoiding a disaster. Let's get started.

YOU ARE YOU

"You are you. Now isn't that pleasant?" That's a quote from the great philosopher Dr. Seuss.

But who are you? This is one of the great questions we all must answer in our lives.

Identifying who we are, to the best of our ability, is a key starting point for executive leadership. And not just who we are as it relates to our position within our organization. We must examine who we are in all areas of life. This will require us to Courageously Ask difficult questions.

Those areas may include our view of self (especially in light of our spiritual view), our view of God, our thoughts on being a spouse and parent, our feelings on things like pride, and our virtues. You may want to consider things like political views and your view on social issues. And yes, who you are as a leader. You may even want to include some attributes that you are striving for.

I strongly encourage anyone who has not done this before, especially executive newbies, to write down this analysis of who you are.

If you do this right, it will take a few days. Anyone who tries to do this in a 10-minute sitting is not doing this assignment justice. Plus, over a few days, you most likely will think of things that you should have included but overlooked.

You are doing this for yourself, so it should be as thorough as possible, with the good, the bad, and the ugly. And if you really want to kick it up a notch, ask your spouse or someone close to you to complete the assignment in regard to you. Compare the lists, but be sure to bring your humility hat.

Put this list in a safe place, or better yet, give it to someone you value who you can trust to hold onto it. The list can even be in a sealed envelope.

Doing this exercise, especially writing it down, will give you a place to go back to when you may have swayed off course based on the pressures of your position and your own weakness.

Rosabeth Moss Kanter, Harvard Business School professor and leadership expert says, "When you fail at something, the best thing to do is think back to your successes, and try to replicate whatever you did to make them happen." This definitely applies to the identification of changes that took place in who you are.

Having something in writing may give us a sober reminder of who we were at a particular point in our lives as we see ourselves falling into a delusion that could be currently besetting us.

I have been doing this exercise for years and have always found that when you have a thoughtfully created baseline to pull out in a time of despair and difficulty, it gives you a jolt. This jolt can motivate you back toward that description of who you truly are. A reset.

Also, many times when people see themselves slipping, or are even way beyond that, they question who they are. I looked in the mirror many times after my fall uttering the words, "Who are you?"

This exercise will definitely help with that.

The leaders I spoke with who found they were able to be themselves— who were most in tune with who they are—most naturally fit into their role of leadership. I consider this group to be among the most successful I interviewed. This comfort was often driven by two things:

1. Their diligent reflection on, and their accurate identification of, who God made them to be. (Although it is mainly geared toward the second half of life, I very successfully used the book *Game Plan* by Bob Buford to identify who God uniquely prepared and designed me to be.)

2. Their ability to make their public/organizational persona consistent with their identity in their private life. As they do this, it allows them to be free of the games we play as we switch who we are, depending on the role we are in.

The two points above take us back to integrity and courage, don't they? We must identify who we honestly are, so that, with integrity, we can hold true to our own self-assessment and have the courage to determine that all of the roles in our lives are going to be consistent with who we are, no matter the cost.

We like to take shortcuts, but this self-assessment is one area where an executive should not take a shortcut. Not analyzing and acting on the two points above is bound to breed misplaced confidence and create insecurity, which will likely result in a lack of assuredness and boldness as the executive works to ensure the advancement and success of the organization. So yes, you are certainly you. And that is pleasant!

IS THAT ME I SEE?

Devoid of consistent, true, humble, and complete self-examination, a Christian nonprofit leader cannot be successful in the long term.

What is your standard?

Your standards help you gauge your strengths, weaknesses, and room for improvement in your self-examination—a reflection of your core values.

If we are not living up to the standard we have set for ourselves (no matter what it is based on), human nature often takes over, and we compare ourselves to a standard we can manipulate.

For instance, if I am not living up to the standard I have set for myself concerning fatherhood, I will compare myself to someone down the street. "Sure, I don't see my children a lot because I get home late from work, but at least I don't travel two weeks out of the month like that guy." Or how about our role at our nonprofit: "No, we are not hitting our fundraising targets this year, but did you hear about the ministry across town? Plus, it's not as bad as last year."

We tend to change the standard to make ourselves feel better, which gives us an inaccurate picture of ourselves. That is why I encourage writing down who you are on paper. It's harder to change a standard that you've written down when you were not in a position of justification.

So, self-examination starts with truth and requires the continued comparison to it.

The late American psychiatrist M. Scott Peck wrote in his book *The Road Less Traveled*, "What does a life of total dedication to truth mean? It means, first of all, a life of continuous and never-ending stringent self-examination. We know the world only through our relationship to it. Therefore, to know the world, we must not only examine it but we must simultaneously examine the examiner."

"Our relationship to it." That would mean that without "never-ending stringent self-examination," we will have great difficulty in relating to the world around us, which would include our role as a nonprofit executive.

As a Christian, self-examination comes with the territory and creates particular standards. There is plenty of scripture dedicated to the command to examine ourselves.

Sometimes it is the person who doesn't acknowledge their weaknesses who is most susceptible to them. Have you acknowledged your weaknesses?

Leaders have a skill for determining the causes of problems and finding solutions to those problems, including HR problems, funding and financial issues, mission focus, community perception, volunteer recruitment, etc. They are skilled at pushing their organizations toward excellence by continually analyzing and solving problems. They spend their day making judgments and decisions about the life of the organization. But do they expend the same energy making judgments and decisions concerning their own life after careful analysis?

At some point, people who recognize the importance of this and make a conscious effort at accomplishing it find that they naturally examine themselves as a part of life.

But that is not everyone, so let's take a look at some ways to get started as you train your mind to do it naturally with very little effort.

There are any number of ways to examine yourself. Personally, my day begins by reading a devotional that starts me off examining myself. *The One-Year Walk with God Devotional* by Chris Tiegreen always gives me at least one aspect of life to focus on in my relationship with God. It only takes me about 10 minutes, but that introspection gets my humility juices flowing as I recognize I have to depend on God to get me through my day unscathed. As a Christian, isn't that what Gospel-centered self-examination comes down to—recognizing your need of Him in all facets of life?

Based on your listing of who you are and who you desire to be, you may want to write down a list of five attributes that you will use in evaluating which direction your life is going. You should be sure to use attributes that cover a wide swath of your life—for instance, professionally, family, spiritually, etc. I recommend changing the list daily or weekly. You may make a commitment to do this at a particular time every day.

Using scripture is another way to examine yourself, as using the standard is always best. For instance, if I am in conflict with someone, I will go to the love verses in 1 Corinthians 13 and place my name in the verse instead of the word love: Brian is patient, Brian is kind, Brian does not boast and is not proud.... Talk about self-examination! It is rare that I read scripture and don't self-evaluate.

Prayer also does the same thing. I am amazed at how many times I pray, and God delivers to me conviction, or my eyes are opened in a particular area of my life.

You may find that you are able to develop a technique that is unique to you and your particular life situation.

While self-examination and evaluation are definitely vital in the life of a Christian leader and are clearly biblically based, a leader needs to make sure they are allowing for balance in the examination, and it is done in a healthy way in light of God's grace and mercy. Remember, Psalms tells us that, "He does not treat us as our sins deserve," and, "He does not repay us for our iniquities." 1 John also tells us, "If we confess our sins He will forgive us and cleanse us of them."

There are many examples out there of highly skilled Christian leaders who so harshly judge their lives and who they are that it brings them down and squelches any faith that may have catapulted them onward and upward in the first place.

Pastor Jared Mellinger writes, "Grace transforms examination from a tyrant and a burden into a means of faith, love, and hope. Self-examination doesn't have to be buckets of water thrown on the fires of our faith. Instead, it can be fuel. We can see where God is at work in us, and we can move forward with the confidence of knowing that He who began a good work in us will bring it on to completion."[29]

There is that principle of balance again.

Proper self-examination takes great humility, even if just within ourselves.

ACCURATE ESTIMATIONS

You are on top of the world. As the founder or leader of your nonprofit organization, you are popular in the community. Everywhere you go you run into someone you know. You are well-respected among your peers and your word carries influence. When politicians and community leaders want to start a new initiative, they call to get your opinion. You are on numerous boards and are invited to be on every committee imaginable. You are a solid Christian who speaks boldly as God is clearly working through you. The money keeps rolling in as people see the need to support the efforts of the organization, many of which you spearheaded. Your family is so proud of you.

You are quick to always give the glory to God and you recognize that your part in all of this is minimal.

Or is it? Sure, you give God credit for all of it, but there is this little part inside of you that says you did answer the call of God. You are the vehicle He chose. It is your signature on all of the documents. It is your name on the awards. You did have a part.

Pride. what a destroyer pride can be!

Without the preservation of humility in the leadership of a successful nonprofit organization, especially one that is Christian in nature, that leadership will find it difficult to inspire a culture of unity, openness, creativity, loyalty, and ultimately, well-rounded success.

Humility is essential in the leadership of any organization, especially a Christian nonprofit.

In fact, this goes way beyond Christian nonprofits. Jim Collins, in his book *Good to Great*, writes that he found two common traits of CEOs in companies that transitioned from average to superior market performance: humility and an indomitable will to advance the cause of the organization.

When it comes to a nonprofit executive taking a proactive approach in preventing their fall, I am going to focus on one quality that must be present in the humility of a leader: the ability to listen.

There is no greater indicator that a leader lacks humility than if that leader does not listen and is not teachable.

When God delivered to me the calling to open a free health clinic as a vehicle to share the Gospel, I had no idea how to do it. Remember I ran grocery stores for many years, so it made no sense. I had a lot to learn.

The only way I was going to be able to do it was to go out to find people who had done it previously and also go to those people who had particular expertise in various areas that were needed to accomplish the task. I even needed personal spiritual guidance. I listened, and I was teachable.

Through his research, Jim Collins discovered that humility and the indomitable will to advance the organization were two common traits of a successful CEO. Sometimes there is friction between those two qualities, and their balance (yes, balance again) is essential in preventing the fall of the individual leader and the organization.

In the beginning, I was humble in my approach to founding the organization through the efforts of tons of people. As the organization got past the first few years, the scale began to tip toward advancement, toward bigger and better things, and I did not listen as much.

I pushed to drive forward, and when people couldn't or wisely wouldn't keep up, I stopped listening.

Humility hung in the balance, sat on the fence.

All of those advisors who were so faithful, whom I allowed in my life, whom I trusted, in my mind became people holding me back and bringing me down.

Some people end up gathering "yes-men and -women" around them so they can push forward their agenda.

Not only did I become skeptical of close advisors, but I started to not listen to myself and the spirit inside me. Self-examination found new standards to measure my life and character against.

Unfortunately, the people around me became weary and gave up, figuring I could handle it all since I kept a smile on everything.

Yes, I was individually accountable for what was happening, but I was falling.

Be humble, listen to wise counsel, slow down, and remain teachable.

I have become a believer who realizes, as a Christian, I cannot fully understand humility unless I fully understand the Gospel. I know, I know—many of you probably think that you understand it. I will tell you that I thought I did as well, until I realized I didn't. Do you fully and deeply understand the Gospel? While I thought I did when I founded the clinic, I now question whether I did or not.

One aspect of humility that needs to be mentioned is the ability to reach out when struggling. Sometimes we see ourselves falling, but many times our pride doesn't allow us to reach out. The fear of looking bad that is part of our human nature takes over, and its power is strong.

There are also times when you reach out and people don't react.

I reached out by telling those closest to me that I was struggling.

My words fell on deaf ears because people thought I could handle it, or they simply did not know what to do. It is your responsibility to shout from the mountaintop if need be. Looking back, I should have not given up and looked for other avenues.

English Baptist preacher Charles Spurgeon once said, "Humility is to make a right estimate of oneself."

The Christian nonprofit executives who are humble and proactive in their accurate estimations of themselves will go a long way in preventing a fall.

NEGLECT = REGRET

Brendan Bridges of Richvale Church in California says, "The things we neglect lead us to a place of regret."

What about the spiritual sacrifices that are made by the deluded, driven executive? If a Christian executive is not taking care of themselves through instruments such as Bible study, devotions, church attendance, family, etc., it's probable the sin nature is going to creep in, waiting for the trigger to turn that sin into an avalanche.

A person who has risen to the level of executive leadership got there through a process. As someone once told me, "Helicopters don't drop people off on top of the mountain of success." God has taken a Christian executive through a process of spiritual awakening, study, trials, and life experiences to get them there. Much of this process involved instruments of growth as described in the previous paragraph.

Too many times the motivation toward these instruments becomes skewed or misplaced as the executive drives toward a goal or sees a modicum of success. Or, frankly, success (as they define it) leaves them feeling as if they do not need those things anymore that got them where they are. Proper humility escapes them.

"When we lead a Christian organization we tend to substitute that [Christian leadership] for real spiritual sustenance. The work becomes your devotions or time with God because you are working full time for God," one nonprofit executive said to me.

He went on to say that during his lowest point in life he wasn't focusing on himself spiritually, and that affected relationships at home with family because he wasn't strengthening his relationship with God. "I was working for God and not with God," he added. "I was punching a clock for God." He said that more than a decade ago he wanted out of his marriage during a time he was working 70–80 hours per week for God without any focus on his own personal relationship with God.

And this is backed up by Pastoralcareinc.com, which notes, "28 percent of pastors report they are spiritually undernourished."[30]

During the time that I started to slide away from my relationship with God, I found myself visiting a different church every week speaking on behalf of the ministry, building awareness of what we were doing. I was missing family small groups, and even my men's group, as I spoke to the same groups in other churches.

Sure, it was good short-term for the ministry God had called me to, but eventually I had no real home church. I had no church home where people were asking, "Where's Brian this week?" They just assumed I was speaking somewhere.

One definite thing that built my faith and strength before founding the clinic was the solid home I had in church with a group of people who held me accountable and made me feel like part of God's family on a human level. That foundation eroded more and more as the organization grew.

Some may say that Christian leaders should be able to stand strong in the Gospel, with the character of the Holy Spirit in us, the sufficiency of God's word, the security of our salvation, and Jesus's exhibited work in our lives. They should be able to depend on God alone for companionship and success.

I would agree, and there are those who are able to do it. But I would also say that there are far too many examples in scripture of how God encouraged fellowship, and not only with Him. Again, we are not perfect, and God knows that better than anyone. In scripture, He always sent out multiples of people together to face difficult challenges. There was a reason for that.

As an executive leader, you did not get to where you are by accident. You worked hard and developed the character traits that your organization desired as they put you in your position. There are specific things that developed that character.

In order to take a proactive approach to preventing a fall, it is time to evaluate those things that developed your character and make sure they still exist in your life.

THE FAMILY BLUR

Sorry, single folks, I am going to focus on those who are married. But you have close family, and you have family who have been with you through thick and thin. So you will most certainly find application here.

In most cases, besides the role of Christ in the life of a leader, the love, support, understanding, and counsel of our spouses have had the biggest influence on who we are at the time of taking the helm of an organization.

Executive leaders regularly take that love, support, understanding, and counsel for granted. This ability to take a partner for granted extends to the rest of the family as well. But the spouse takes the brunt.

You may remember back in Chapter 4, as I highlighted executive struggles, I noted that an executive cannot expect their spouse to understand what they are going through. This is true and part of human nature, but many times that human nature is simply protecting its territory as the affections and time of their spouse is allowed to be stolen by the nonprofit. And remember, to an executive's spouse, the executive is a spouse first. The nonprofit executive part is much lower on the list of properly prioritized roles in the life of their spouse.

And rightfully so. Driven executives get this backward many times as they find their main focus to be on organizational goals. Everything else is a blur, including the very family who gave them the stability to take risks and rise to the level they currently reside in.

Rosabeth Moss Kanter says, "Ambivalence about family responsibilities has a long history in the corporate world." And, certainly, this same ambivalence stretches into the nonprofit world. Executives are torn.

Many leaders have difficulty prioritizing their time. They assume that their family has the same passion they do concerning the mission and is willing to sacrifice right along with them. Guess what? Sometimes they aren't.

I can remember my wife crying out numerous times: "Why did God not give me the same calling as you, so that we could have the same drive and passion for what is being created?"

One time when there were struggles at home, I had a good friend challenge me by Courageously Asking if God called me to be a solid husband and father first, or a nonprofit CEO first. "Which was the higher priority?" he asked. As I sat across the lunch booth that day, the answer was quite obvious. But nothing changed, and I kept right on going, assuming my family understood the "higher" purpose. I was wrong!

I fell. Not only did I fall, but I fell in a way that was an insult to the family who provided the support that allowed me to follow my calling, which became my dream.

Remember, most falls come under the category of "moral failure."

There is no one closer to the challenges in your life that fall into that category than your spouse.

Executive, listen to your spouse. And not just what they are saying. They communicate in many ways. Use the knowledge you have gained in being a student of your spouse as you watch and listen to them. They see things you don't.

Giving and maintaining the proper place of your family in your life goes a long way in being proactive to prevent a fall that starts with a tiny crack that can quickly become an avalanche.

SPEED BUMPS

I was recently reading the book *Too Small to Ignore* by Wes Stafford, the former 20-year president of Compassion International. It's a very good book that takes you through his life as a missionary child in Western Africa and how it prepared him for his presidency of a large multinational nonprofit.

At one point in the book, Wes tells a story about him and his father traveling the roads of the Ivory Coast (also known as Côte d'Ivoire) in their old pickup truck. He told of how they would see large boa constrictors stretched across the road making it difficult to see which end contained a head and which end contained a tail. He ends the story with, "Talk about a speed bump!"

All of us have traveled over speed bumps. They are common in parking lots and neighborhoods. Most people probably don't even think about speed bumps until they run over one a little too fast, or they are in a hurry and encounter one.

Many times people take drastic measures to avoid them, swerving to one side so only two tires hit them or none at all. Or they won't travel in an area where they know a speed bump is located.

We don't want to slow down. We want to keep going, full speed ahead, even if the speed bump could cause long-term damage.

I am no different than anyone else in that I hate speed bumps, even though I drive an SUV.

Unfortunately, many leaders, and people in general, also hate speed bumps. However, most times this loathing of speed bumps has nothing to do with a car.

Allow me to explain. When a legitimately concerned person who is in solid relationship with a leader (friend, board member, spouse, congregant, etc.) approaches a leader with loving constructive criticism or a concern and that leader blows them off without genuine consideration, that's a speed bump. The leader just keeps rolling, not recognizing the damage that has been done on several fronts.

Think about the parallels. Just like in a car, the speed at which a leader rolls over the speed bump determines if it might profit them and those around them, or if it causes damage. If a person drives over speed bumps at a high rate of speed, damage will eventually be done to the vehicle as the parts rattle apart and undue wear occurs. If a person, especially a leader, continues to roll over the advice of those closest to them at a high rate of speed, eventually damage will be done.

A speed bump is intended to slow a vehicle down for a variety of reasons. Many times a leader reacts so quickly to advice that is given to them—sometimes automatically on the defensive—that an hour later they have to reconsider their reaction. We have all done it, given into that first impulse that we regret later. Damage is caused. We have blown right over the speed bump.

How in the world do you have time to capture every thought and make it obedient (2 Corinthians 10:5) if you blow right by that opportunity? Leaders struggle with this because they think they have to have a quick, decisive answer to everything. And then there is that darn pride thing. This is especially true when they are confronted about something within themselves.

However, if a leader is able to see the indicators that a speed bump is in front of them and has the desire and ability to slow down, there just might be some opportunity for growth in the experience. This is not easy for the driven, results-oriented leader. In fact, many will say that it is impossible. Yet, it is vital.

I used to have a terribly sinful anger issue. There is no doubt that it came from my childhood and that it was based in arrogance, fear, and insecurity. It was so automatic and happened so naturally. I had trained myself on how to react to certain things with anger as if it was the same as pulling my hand off a hot stove. It would usually pop up when I was losing control of a situation or I was feeling emotional pain. It was my way of taking control. As a young adult, I would say that it was just "part of who I am," as if I had no responsibility for it.

I learned about individual accountability, and guess what? All of my excuses for anger went out the window. So, I developed strategies that helped me to recognize when it was coming, what to do in the situation, and where to set my focus. It always involved saying a very quick prayer. Every single time I did, the Holy Spirit would send to me a scripture that I had memorized around the issue. And I was able to go over the speed bump slowly and not cause damage.

It is possible. I ask you to examine your own heart in whatever sin has become "automatic" in light of this. From out of the mouth the heart speaks (Matthew 12:34).

Who doesn't try to avoid a speed bump in their car? Sometimes avoiding conversations that have the potential to turn into a speed bump in relationships do as much damage as running over a speed bump at a high rate of speed. Avoiding this type of conversation can take us to the land of assumption I discussed in Chapter 3.

To think we have all the answers is a sin. To think we don't need other people to help us on our journey is just plain a mistake.

Without being able to listen to trusted people who love you and continually speed-bumping the advice that comes your way, damage will eventually be done to you and those around you. Approachability goes down, and your number one resource in the form of other people is shunted. This is when a leader may become vulnerable to a fall.

Although some of the responsibility of revealing what a person sees in the life of a leader falls on those around the leader, it is ultimately the leader's responsibility to accept what they are saying and strongly consider it against what they may think.

It is up to the leader to continually decide which advisors to let into their inner circle, what advice is legitimate, and what advice is detrimental. It is the wisdom to be able to properly discern this that separates a great leader from a good leader.

The wisdom to do this starts with the ability to listen to all people with significant attention and to leave them validated without feeling like a speed bump. If I could only go back in my life and flatten out some of those speed bumps, or slow down as I approached them, my life would be quite different.

I started this chapter speaking about individual accountability. This is just another area where the leaders themselves have to make the choice of humility before those whom God sends to us to help us on our journey.

Or do we want to keep trucking forward with car parts, broken relationships, and missed opportunities in the dust behind us?

THE BOARD WANTS YOU TO BE SUCCESSFUL

Executive, you know each member of your board. In fact, it is doubtful that anyone on your board would have been elected to your board if you did not approve. Each member of your board was chosen, usually with your input, for a particular reason. They bring something to the board and the organization that is desirable and needed.

On the flipside, the board either chose to serve with you or chose you as the executive because they believed in you.

Legally, the board is the entity, and as such, it is responsible for the success or failure of the organization. They get to celebrate with you or clean up right along with you, and sometimes without you. It's a big responsibility, and they are your boss.

In most cases, each member of your board is a volunteer. They are serving at their own will because they have a passion for the organization you represent and serve. This passion drives them to want to contribute, and one of the ways they do that is through their board membership. They are sacrificing time they could be using for other important parts of their life, including family time. They came on the board because they believe in the organization.

So, what do you do with all of that?

You respect it.

It's imperative to work hard to develop the best relationships possible with each individual board member. They ended up on your board because of their wisdom, and you need to avail yourself of that wisdom, even if it hurts at times.

Many times the survival of a floundering executive can be affected by board members who, like all of us, are imperfect, fallible people. They deserve the same degree of grace and mercy that you demand from them.

As I look back, I have to say that there was no time before, during, or after my fall that I found myself wondering if my board wanted me to be successful. We certainly did not agree on how each other handled things during the difficult times, but I have found that with time and the proper application of grace, I am able to see things much clearer and come to this conclusion.

Executive, your relationship with your board is one that needs to be nurtured in a purposeful way. They need to be your partner when you are experiencing success and when you are struggling. You need to be able to entrust them with both, even when the struggle delves into an area deemed personal.

I would strongly recommend taking the level of relationship with one or more of them to a deeper level than the rest. This will require vulnerability, trust, and a high level of courage.

My wife and I have found ourselves looking for a home church a time or two. I would say there are at least 50 churches within 15 minutes of our home. As I have gotten older, I have realized that if we cannot find a church that fits within our needs and standards, we are probably the problem.

If an executive cannot develop a high level of relationship with one of at least five board members, it might be time for some introspection.

Never underestimate the importance of the relationship you have with your board. It is as important as any relationship you have related to your organization. That includes volunteers, staff, donors, government officials, accountants, and everyone else. In fact, most times your relationship with the board is most important.

The best long-term leaders avail themselves of all the resources they have around them. Many times they have built a bank of resources that have gotten them to their current position. That bank of resources usually includes close family and mentors, books by inspiring authors including the Bible, routines, and personal habits.

The number one resource is the bank of character traits that has been built within the executive. For Christians, what is built within them is the Holy Spirit and the knowledge of the Gospel, and these solidify them.

Leadership at an executive level has the great capability of pulling us from those things that supported us as we rose to that level, even as we followed a calling. That pull can cause a fall of avalanche proportions.

I once heard leadership expert John Maxwell say that it is impossible to enjoy sustained success without self-discipline and that his greatest leadership challenge is "leading me."

Executive, it is time to ask yourself if you are ready to lead yourself to a life of self-discipline that will give you sustained success, not only in your professional life, but in your life as a whole.

I think you are ready.

Leader, it's time for you to be proactive.

CHAPTER 7

BUT, THE BOARD HAS A ROLE

A SOLID RELATIONSHIP between executive and board that encompasses *all* of whom the leader is, and the various roles they play inside and outside of an organization is possible, but is unfortunately rare. The ability of an accountability structure—here we will mainly address a board of directors—to communicate their care for their executive through the appropriate involvement in their personal life, as well as their job description, can be the difference between success and a leadership fall that many times culminates in organizational struggle.

My interviews and personal experience on boards of directors tell me that the role of the board in the personal life of an executive will be questioned.

This chapter will address what an appropriate relationship, beyond the job description, is with a nonprofit executive.

You may be part of that rare relationship. Frankly, I have witnessed this rare relationship with my own eyes, both as an outsider and as a board member.

Many board members will say that the relationship they have with their executive is what it should be and is solid. If that is your answer, I would ask you a couple questions:

1. Has the relationship been tested through adversity? So many times after adversity strikes, an organization recognizes that the relationship was not as strong as they had hoped. Many times, when the facts come out, a board recognizes things they should have known, and would have known, had the relationship been stronger, had they been paying attention. But many times it's too late.

2. What would the opinion of your executive be? Just asking them the question is not good enough. Probe. Ask follow-up questions. Press the issue. Every executive wants to get along with their board, but they are not so quick to answer a question or assertion like this with complete honesty because of fear. There are executives reading this right now who would love for their board to ask them how they view the board-executive relationship and be able to answer with complete honesty.

But here is the real question you should be asking: even if Brian is wrong, is an exploration concerning the benefits of a closer, more personal relationship worth the effort?

If you have gotten this far in the book you recognize that a fall could happen in your organization. You recognize what harm could be done to your organization if you are caught not paying attention to more than a job description. You realize that even if an executive falls due to a core personal issue, the organizational problem and the recovery from it falls in your lap.

Long ago, before I fell and when I was leading our free health clinic, I recognized the need for a board to look beyond a job description in evaluating the effectiveness of their executive.

I was seeing issues all around me and in my own experience when it came to the board-executive relationship. But even as I wrote this book I thought I might be taking too hard of a stance concerning the volunteer board of directors. So, I started asking around.

I asked a strong natural leader and the organization founder of a midsize ($3.3 million) organization if she thought I might be a little too hard on the board side of things. Her organization has done it right, and this leader has other board experience. The response I received was this: "There are many resources out there developed for teaching a leader how to create a culture in an organization that breeds transparency, openness, and empowerment; a culture that values the individual as a human being and not just as a worker with a job description." This leader continued by saying, "This hasn't hit the boardroom yet and is a challenge of our time."

Wow, I was taken aback. I couldn't have said it better myself.

So, let's move that needle.

IT CAN HAPPEN

I recently met with the CEO of a $10+ million organization who has been in his position for over 30 years. That many years would encompass many different boards and board chairs. He has had mostly good experiences with the boards he has worked with. This executive can remember many stories over the years of boards treating him well.

From the growing pains of being a new CEO, to his wife being sick with cancer, to his son being deployed to Iraq, to a major legal challenge in his role as CEO, he can relate stories of how his board supported him in both personal and professional ways. He can remember them giving him the leeway that was needed, while protecting the organization. Most of those are normal life issues that any board would be supportive through.

But a few years back this leader found himself named in charges related to one of the participants at a camp their organization operated.

The case was public, and it was being judged all throughout the community. Everyone was talking about it.

Think of the various parts of his life, in his mind, that were splintering and spreading just like a chip in a windshield, at breakneck speed. The legacy he had worked so hard for over those many years with the organization was at stake. His reputation as a solid, upstanding community leader was in jeopardy.

Questions swirled in his head: What do people think of me? What are the organization's employees thinking? Will I lose all that I have worked for? My gosh, will I have to serve time? Most importantly, what do my three children and wife think? Am I honoring God? All of this pressure kept building and building.

From day one, the executive and the organization denied any culpability in the case. But there were definitely questions concerning his leadership. Some were saying that there was a failure of leadership. Self-doubt set in as the executive analyzed and judged every decision that was made.

The community as a whole was not sure which way this was going to go. There was confusion, and loyalties were questioned and sometimes broken.

The community watched the potential fall of a well-respected CEO and the damage of a solid organizational reputation.

Eventually all charges were dismissed, all records were expunged, and the leader returned to work after about four months.

For the purposes of this book, it is not necessary to dig into the details of this case. It is, however, important to examine the treatment of the leader by the board from the CEO's perspective.

I said that this could have gone either way. There was no slam dunk on either side. As the situation sent shock waves throughout the community, the 24-member board had to weigh everything and make decisions that would not only protect the organization, but show the community the character of the organization and the board that governed it.

Concerning how the leader was treated: he remembers meetings in his living room with the board chair and other members of the executive committee that found each of them tearing up as they discussed the options. They paid him during the four-month leave of absence and were there for him when they were needed. They went so far as to hire a very well-qualified interim CEO while he was gone in order to ensure continuity in the organization.

The relationship between board and executive was on display for all to see. The caring attitude of the board toward the CEO was quite apparent.

And what was created by all of this wisdom and support throughout the unfortunate process? Loyalty. In the words of this CEO, "I was going to make it up to them. I determined that, God willing, I would retire from this organization if they will continue to have me. My wife and I changed our will in order to give back all of the pay that was given to me during the leave of absence in multiples." Loyalty.

The board acted with wisdom, supporting the leader the whole way through until the end. They did not jump the gun in judgment and had a relationship with this CEO that allowed them to trust him until the facts showed otherwise. That relationship does not just happen, and I will discuss that a little later.

Think about if the board would have gone the other way. What if they had jumped to judgment, acting in fear as the case was playing out in the court of public opinion? What if they had immediately disciplined him, succumbed to the pressures of the opposition, and maybe even terminated him? What if they would have put out a statement that protected the organization, but left the leader out in the cold?

I ask these questions because I have seen these things happen.

The answer to most of these questions can be summed up in just a few sentences. The organization would not have a dedicated leader with such a deep passion for the success of the organizational mission.

They would have prevented God's discipline on this leader in the area of legacy. As the CEO said to me, "I know God was working in me to show me that it was about His legacy and not my prideful legacy."

Other organizations would not have benefited from this story that shows wisdom in the face of heavy community criticism.

But most importantly, the community saw a Godly example in the form of this board's bold reaction to adversity and the treatment of its leader.

This did not happen by coincidence or by accident.

THE STICKY RESPONSIBILITY

In the world of nonprofit board responsibilities, treating the executive in a way that allows them to be human must be elevated. If an executive is not successful personally as well as professionally, the organization will eventually suffer.

It is easy to list "accountability of the executive" or "executive evaluation" on a list of board responsibilities. It is even easier to then follow with a list of particular points of accountability and parameters for their performance.

For board members, it gets harder when they have to evaluate the executive on performance goals that are not tangible or numbers oriented.

It's so easy to analyze data points and financial goals. Most of these are simply black and white, success or failure. Holding a leader accountable to a set of parameters is so much easier than getting down in the muck of their personal life. But most of the time the muck is where leadership falls find their origin. And the issues ultimately end up in the lap of the board. This is where it gets sticky and uncomfortable for board members.

Some would say that the personal life of an executive should not be taken into consideration when measuring the effectiveness of that leader while evaluating their performance.

But the personal life of an executive is going to affect their performance.

Who a person is—the way they were brought up, their education, their faith life, their life experiences, etc.—forms the foundation of that leader and made them who you chose to lead your organization. That is very personal.

The reason a board chooses a particular executive cannot just be found on the sheets of paper we call a résumé. If that were true, there would be no reason for interviews.

When a board conducts interviews, they are looking for character and personality. They are looking for indicators of proper application of the skills they find on the résumé. They are searching to see if this person can create or maintain the desired culture, and so on. These are mostly intangible and without measurable performance indicators.

This begs the question, if we are hiring someone based on their professional capabilities as well as their personal traits that will help drive the organization forward in a way we desire, why are we not nurturing and monitoring that humanness? It's hard. It's sticky.

Yet, it has to be done, or we risk the organization's well-being. Board members have to ask themselves if they have the courage to do the uncomfortable: To consciously, purposefully engage the leader in an effort to protect them from being in a position, no matter how they got there, that jeopardizes the organization. To value the leader as a human being, allow them to be vulnerable, and even fallible.

To dig deep with them, and help protect them from attacks, even attacks that they seemingly initiate.

As we have already reviewed, the costs to a board are quite high when they are not being proactive in helping to protect an executive from the temptations that may leave them as a shell of themselves.

Hopefully those who take a hardline approach and desire to stick with the tangible parameters of accountability are now seeing what I see and many have experienced: without a conscious effort by the accountability structure as a whole to care for the leader in a responsible, but personally compassionate way, the personal issues that are harbored by many executives will end up in the lap of the board.

It's really hard to be critical of boards when it comes to this kind of thing because this is just how things have always been done in the nonprofit world. But a fundamental change must take place.

In too many cases, because the executive leader was called and has shown great faith in carrying out their work, the board feels that the executive is shielded from the same practical concerns about life that they themselves have. Somehow this is all part of the supernatural calling and provision of God. And that somehow makes it okay.

That is not always consciously done. Board members are living their own lives, dealing with their own life issues. They are almost always volunteers, for Pete's sake.

My hope, though, is to raise the level of sensitivity toward the individual executive personally to the level of any other responsibility a board member has in fulfilling their fiduciary duty.

Again, these are pretty strong statements. Pretty strong until you consider that the fall of a nonprofit organizational executive can be as damaging to the organization as any failure listed in the duties of a board of directors or in an executive job description.

What hurts an organization more: missing the year-end budget by 20 percent or the organization experiencing the ugly, public fall of their executive? Should be an easy answer.

A board cannot afford to knowingly allow a fall to happen, even if its prevention is sticky.

Taking a proactive approach in developing a relationship between the board and executive is an absolute key in the prevention of a fall. Sometimes the level of that relationship can even be deep enough that the board finds they may be saving the leader from themselves.

It can happen.

It's time to open up the conversation.

SAVE THE LEADER FROM WHOM?

Let's go back to the boardroom the day I revealed that I was involved in a three-month emotional affair. Remember how the one board member looked at me and asked, "What part of your issue did [our organization] play?"

After a few years of healing following my fall, I went back to that same board member to inquire as to why they asked that question.

Their answer: "Because I had sensed for months that something was not right, my question was shaded with a bit of introspection as to what we, and more pointedly me, as a board could have done to help you from falling into sin."

All along, the board could have been consciously and proactively saving me from myself. Does that make it their fault? Absolutely not. But they could have helped. They could have Courageously Asked the right questions of me. Instead of simply accepting my answer of "good" or "very good" when they asked me how I was doing, they could have probed further and followed their gut instinct.

They could have asked the right questions of my wife and those closest to me.

I was driven and willing to sacrifice anything for the success of the ministry. Sure, I would put it on God's calling, but we humans sometimes take things to their extreme, way beyond where God intends us to go. That was me.

In Chapter 4, I wrote about the struggles executives deal with in their role. This is a perfect example of being able to use the perspective of another role in the organization.

So, one question might be: "Would the leader listen?" Maybe, maybe not. Pride is a crazy thing. This should not be a consideration. A board has the responsibility to broach the topic and express concerns, no matter the origin of the concern. If the executive does not receive the board's concerns, the board, in a worst-case scenario, must use their authority to make sure they do.

These things are so much easier if there is a relationship based on trust and care for the executive. This is one example of why it is so important to be proactive when dealing with issues and concerns.

Saving a leader from themselves is an art and takes just the right relationship, developed over time before any issues, in order for both to walk away happy and respected. A board member cannot just go to an executive and declare that there is going to be an improved relationship between them and the executive.

Boards, it's time to talk about it, and act.

WHERE IT BEGINS

Believe it or not, the relationship between the board and the executive starts before they are even hired. As the board sits around the table working to determine the profile of their ultimate candidate, many times what are considered are things like education, past experience, community involvement, standing in the community, expertise in the particular mission, fundraising potential, demonstrated ability to create and maintain culture, and general personal stability. This is typical, and each one of those points is very important. They are all "musts."

But what you have already learned is that I am imploring boards to go the extra step. Perhaps we should also be pushing the envelope on the personal side of life. Although some candidates will be scared off by that, it is okay. What you are looking for is someone who has the character that allows them to be the same person in your organization as they are at home or in other settings. If they protect that, it may be an indicator that they are not your ideal candidate.

As a board is looking for their ideal candidate and developing their executive profile, the board is in the driver's seat. This needs to be taken very seriously, and a board should take their time—be wary of those speed bumps on the road.

Too many times a board is so anxious to fill a position and get on with business as usual that they rush the process, cut corners, and choose the wrong candidate. Sometimes a board will put someone in a position because they are the easiest one to get up and running fast. This is not a wise decision-making process.

Asking questions around a person's holistic health should not be off the table.

What I am advocating for, in the interest of the health of your organization, is for you to have the courage to probe areas of a candidate's personal life. A board should be looking for indications that a solid relationship can be built between board and executive and that the candidate not only possesses strength and ability, but also humility.

There are certainly things that you cannot legally ask a candidate, but there are many you can. So, asking about personal interests outside of the job and what they do with their time should be probed. You are looking to uncover the leader's mindset and personal state. In a missional Christian organization, asking what their church involvement is and about affiliations is relevant. Asking if they attend a small accountability group is a good question. Asking about life challenges and how they handled them—now we're talking. Inevitably, questions like these will lead to further discussion on topics relevant to your Christian mission.

Time and time again I have heard people talk about how proper vetting of leadership is so important. The problem is that many times they are talking about this after the fall.

Going back to my experience on the board where we asked for the executive's resignation, it was amazing how many people sat around that table (including me) talking about the indicators we saw before they were even put in the position. We all saw it but took the easy route and put them in the position. Lesson learned.

Proper vetting of a potential executive by asking personal questions in a gentle, caring way during the interview process also has a few side effects. First, it tells the candidate something about the character of the board and the organization. It also shows a part of the character of the organization that you want incorporated as part of the culture of the organization when they carry out their duties.

It will communicate to them that they are cared about on a personal level, beyond the facts and figures that you no doubt will have reviewed as part of the job description review. That is very attractive to your ideal candidates and may be the reason they choose your organization over others.

And this same attitude should be seen in the onboarding of the new candidate. The board should develop a deliberate, purposeful onboarding process headed up by at least one board member.

A solid, healthy, and communicative relationship starts before the hiring of an executive. Do not take it for granted.

No matter where the board-executive relationship begins, whether it be during the hiring process or sometime during the executive's tenure, properly communicated expectations that are well thought out and reasonable, considering the individual, are essential.

EXPECTATIONS

Expectations are real. Expectations are needed. Expectations inspire. Expectations motivate.

Expectations within a nonprofit organization run the gamut, applying to a wide array of relationships: the board's expectations of the executive, the executive's expectations of the board, and expectations in the relationships between staff, volunteers, donors, and community.

Some expectations are very clearly documented, but there are many more that are unwritten and are based in human nature, tradition, and commonly held practices.

Because we all come from different backgrounds and traditions, the unwritten expectations sometimes lead us to the land of assumption.

Because some expectations are not clearly communicated, and sometimes can't be, an executive will assume them, thereby creating a high level of pressure as they try to fulfill not only the communicated expectations but those that are assumed.

And difficulties arising from the land of assumption usually find their solution in increased communication.

Sometimes all of the factors that form the expectations of the executive—written expectations as well as those created through human nature, tradition, and commonly held practice—come together. But too many times they come together without the thoughtful consideration of the board and those around the executive. An attitude of "this is the way we have always done it" takes the place of that thoughtful consideration.

Allow me to give you an example in the life of an executive pastor. I recently attended Easter services with a friend in the next town. Although I knew people in this congregation and the pastor, I had never attended a service at this mainline denominational church.

After some small talk with people I knew, I entered the church and sat in a pew with my friend. As most visitors do, I opened the bulletin to learn a little about the service and what was going on at the church. I opened the bulletin, and on the first page, I found this declaration in a box taking up almost half of the first page:

PASTORAL SUPPORT AND VISITS

Rev. XXXXX is available twenty-four hours a day, seven days a week to provide you and your family with the spiritual support and comfort needed during illness, accidents, hospitalizations, family emergencies, etc.

In order to ensure that Rev. XXXXX can provide pastoral support for emergencies on a timely basis, please call his home phone (xxx-xxx-xxxx) rather than the pastor's office phone. If you reach his phone mail, please leave your name, telephone number, and a brief message, and he will return your call as quickly as possible. Rev. XXXXX will, in turn, notify the appropriate church member(s) regarding the specific situation.

Sounds like exactly what you would expect a humble servant leader to say. This pastor clearly is laying down his life for Christ and is His ambassador here on earth. Isn't this exactly what you would expect Jesus himself to say or do? In fact, I brought it home to my wife and she thought it was nice of them to put his home number in the bulletin.

Now, if I wasn't reading this bulletin at the time of the writing of this book I would have blown right by it. In fact, I probably would have been impressed, if I paid any attention at all. But I guess because I have been talking to Christian leaders for some time about what they are struggling with, this bold statement stopped me in my tracks. Immediately I started asking myself the following questions:

1. Is this guy superhuman?

2. What does his family think of this?

3. Who wrote it?

4. Did an unknowing church member write it?

5. Is this really the expectation of him?

6. Did he write it thinking that was the expectation of him?

Hmm... According to Pastoralcareinc.com:

- 84% of pastors feel they are on call 24/7,

- 78% of pastors report having their vacation and personal time interrupted with ministry duties or expectations,

- 80% of pastors believe their ministry has negatively affected their families,

- 65% of pastors feel their family lives in a glass house and fear they are not good enough to meet expectations, and

- 52% of pastors feel overworked and cannot meet their church's unrealistic expectations.

These few statistics clearly spell out the fact that pastors feel as if the expectations placed on them create pressures that make it difficult for them to maintain proper family relationships and promote difficulties within themselves.

Each category of executive leadership in the nonprofit world has its own challenges, and being a pastor is no different.

So, let's turn this around a little bit. We all know that Christian leadership is unique and that God strengthens those who act on His calling to the ministry. But Christian leaders are human beings too. Can you imagine if your vocation posted to all of the customers of your company that you were available 24/7? How would you react?

I eventually spoke to this particular executive leader about the bulletin. He had been in the ministry for about 40 years. In the beginning of our conversation he took a very sincere, noble approach. He told me that he wrote it and that he and his wife knew of this expectation going in. He said that, for his age and for pastors from his era, the expectations are reasonable.

But he said the differences in generations are big. He said that the younger men and women are drawing a line in the sand concerning personal time. He actually respects them for doing it and wishes he would have had the "gumption" to do it when he was younger. He went on to say, "This more principled approach to time allocation can only be good for the ministry, as the pastor's family thrives through the protection of family time."

As the interview went on, he discussed the many ways a congregation expects that all of his time is their time, and they tend to treat it as such. He told me stories of people stopping in his office without an appointment while he was working.

Now, he was sure to acknowledge the pastoral duty inherent in his vocation and was gracious in his descriptions.

But there was no question that the expectations sometimes frustrated him.

This Easter experience and the interview that followed cemented in my mind that executive leaders desire to be a particular person, this ideal, to fulfill what they perceive as the expectations.

This is very desirable and noble, but can be pressure packed and humanly frustrating.

Written expectations are known, accepted, and signed off on by both parties. It's pretty easy.

But the unwritten expectations that come from human nature, tradition, and common practices create assumptions, which create undue pressure, sometimes driving the image an executive has of their job performance into the ground.

It is the job of the board to manage the expectations of the executive, sometimes even protecting them from unreasonable expectations from the board itself. The board can also go a long way in protecting them from others in the executive's sphere of influence.

Communication of clearly laid out expectations, which would include written and unwritten expectations (to the best of their ability), is absolutely vital in the quest for a solid board-executive relationship.

The solidifying of this relationship by communicating clear and complete expectations will make a huge difference in proactively creating a culture that prevents a leadership fall.

One expectation that can create confusion, and sometimes friction, is the expectation of board engagement in the organization. This is an expectation that is rarely laid out clearly, thereby leading both the executive and the board to the land of assumption.

LET'S GET ENGAGED

According to the National Council of Nonprofits, "An engaged board is a forward-thinking board that strives to have a collaborative partnership with the CEO/executive director, which means partnering for fundraising, as well as policy-making. Engaged boards 'work' between board meetings, and attend meetings well prepared.

They are willing to deliberate candidly, confidently treading on sensitive topics that may result in 'messy' discussions because they trust one another and are comfortable with the culture of the nonprofit, confident that everyone values mutual respect."[31]

So, there you have it. An excellent description of a properly engaged board. I would only add to the description the need for a properly engaged board to be involved in the life of their executive at an appropriate level.

The description is well rounded and hits nearly all of the key points. Of the numerous boards I have served on, I would say maybe three have come close to the mark described above. That leaves many needing improvement.

Board engagement is critical. It is not only critical to the operation and growth of the organization, it is important to the executive on a personal level. Board engagement transforms the declaration of board support into action, which makes the words of the board much more impactful and sincere. This helps an executive move forward with boldness and confidence.

There are few things more important that a board can do in being proactive in preventing the fall of a nonprofit executive than being engaged. The relationship between the executive and their accountability structure is heavily influenced by the amount of board engagement the executive experiences. Nearly every nonprofit executive I interviewed said as much.

And really, to the executive, any type of sincere board engagement is typically magnified in their mind, and it lifts their spirit as they feel genuinely supported. Yes, there are those executives that are very demanding, whom a board cannot do enough for. But they are rare.

One executive I interviewed said that 80–90 percent of emails they send out to the board do not garner a reply. They went on to say, "Simple responses like 'Thanks for sharing that info,' or 'We'll be praying for that,' or even 'How can I pitch in?' would have made a huge difference." To this executive, it would be just that simple. They said that many times they would send a follow-up email a few days later because they thought there may have been a computer glitch.

Another executive of a large nonprofit I interviewed said of their board, "A majority come to one meeting per month, if they come. Even then, they don't ask how I am but just ask 'How are the numbers?'"

And still another said, "It would be earth shattering to have a board member pop into the office once in a while."

I have interviewed leaders who, in the interest of the organization's mission, forego raises or even paychecks so they can increase staff or even simply make sure the staff gets paid when things are tight.

One of the CEOs of a million-dollar nonprofit I interviewed told me that during tough times a year or two ago he was holding nine paychecks that he would not cash so employees would get paid. Did the board even know this?

I know in my case that the board tried to give me a raise twice, and I said no. I told them to give me more vacation, which, of course, I never took.

In my experience, most executives crave board engagement.

All organizations need board engagement. You'll notice that none of the actions mentioned above take much time.

As described above, one of the biggest benefits to board engagement is the manifestation of a board declaration into a genuine, active declaration. But there is one more big benefit.

Increased board engagement, and especially increased engagement with the executive, gives the board a clearer view of the organization and the leader. This could not only help the board to carry out their fiduciary responsibilities but could help them to monitor the leader on professional and personal levels. This will help identify issues and even personal activities that may be triggers in an impending fall.

One nonprofit executive I interviewed said, "A board needs to be known by their engagement. If a board is known in the community and by going to events, the typical participant in those events knows who to go to if they see a problem. This increases the eyes of the board and can prevent a leadership fall by catching something earlier."

Another multimillion-dollar nonprofit CEO with decades of board experience said, "If a board is really focused on mission and governance, and strategically working with a senior leader on those areas, they would probably get into a lot of things the leader is struggling with. The board chair would help run the board side. They know what the leader wants to get done and would know where there would be board obstacles and they work the system. Team approach. This creates relationship."

Too many times something catastrophic happens in an organization that leaves a board wondering how they did not see it or see it coming. They are dumbfounded. They realize they were not paying attention. This can be alleviated by increased board engagement.

A board member who struggles in their motivation to be adequately engaged in an organization they have chosen to be part of should examine if they should indeed be part of the board of that organization. Maybe they have lost their initial passion, but it may be a matter of timing concerning other temporary, more important circumstances in the life of the board member.

Of course, too much board engagement can also be damaging, as it may be perceived as micromanagement. This may actually lower the executive's confidence in their own abilities.

Appropriate board engagement is different in each organization and is based on things like the age of the organization, the history of the organization, past practices, and the experience and personality of the executive.

But just remember, the board hired their particular executive for a reason. The executive must be allowed to manage the organization.

One bank CEO turned philanthropist and active board member I know tells of the two questions he asks as he leads nonprofit boards he serves on:

1. Is the executive the right person for the job?

2. If the answer to question number one is yes, what can we do to support them in their position?

He says that these two questions help them focus their board engagement.

Most boards will recognize they need to step up their game when it comes to being more engaged in the organization they are so passionate about. It may be time to act on that recognition.

But what about being engaged in the life of the executive?

BOARD ENGAGEMENT
IN THE LIFE OF THE EXECUTIVE

I would argue that managing the threat of a personally dysfunctional executive overrides nearly every properly functioning responsibility of a board of directors. This threat, and paying attention to it, should garner the board's consideration more than any other.

As has been discussed previously, your executive is a person, a human being with feelings, emotions, joys, hurts, and pains outside the leadership role they are in. Should they be able to manage that part of their life? Sure they should. That is one reason you picked them to lead your organization. But each person has their ups and downs, struggles and difficulties.

Many times we expect our executives to be superhuman but forget that there is no "super" without the "human." Even strong executives are going to fall short at times. The desire of a board should be to make sure they know a struggle is coming as early as possible so they may be able to react to a seemingly small trigger before it becomes an avalanche of destruction.

This is done by going beyond the board duty of holding an executive accountable to a job description. I've already written about this at length, so I will not belabor the point.

Each organization, board, and executive, along with the relationships that govern them, are different, so there is no simple five-step plan that is sure to stave off a fall. But I would like to propose a few suggestions.

First of all, be proactive as a board and talk about issues that arise. Perform a Courageous Ask. Don't shove them to the side just because your executive appears steady at this particular point in your organization's history. Your goal, above almost anything else, should be to help keep them on solid ground.

You chose to read beyond Chapter 1, so you recognized the potential for a leadership fall is real. Talk about it as a board and with the executive. Make the private life of your executive part of board discussions, with and without the executive present. It's easy to talk about the financial reports, but a misstep or failure in the personal life of the executive could be just as damaging to the organization. So, talk about it.

While insisting on open communication concerning the personal life of your executive, determine with that executive what is too intrusive. Do this while things are good, so the level of monitoring is made by objective parties.

The board will have to determine if the agreement is satisfactory and helps in the integrity of the relationship. If not, the board needs to be honest with the executive and ask for more. This may or may not be satisfactory to the executive. If not, the board and the executive have a decision to make. Remember, the board will ultimately end up with both successes and failures falling in their laps, and the board is ultimately in charge as the guardian of the entity.

Let me remind you, I am not talking about an all-encompassing intrusion into the private life of an executive. I am talking about a balanced monitoring based on a solid relationship between the board and executive; a monitoring that communicates that the board cares for the executive not only as a person filling a job description but as an individual.

Examples of areas in the personal life of an executive needing to be probed should include foundational areas that made the executive the board's chosen candidate. Included would be areas such as family relationships, spiritual life and spiritual disciplines, and community involvement. Also needing to be addressed should be areas of pressure and areas where the leader is feeling insecure. These suggestions should provide a starting point.

Again, sincerity in the care of the executive is key. The board must choose the right person or people to perform this function.

The whole board does not need to be involved. Ideally, the board chair has a relationship with the executive that allows for this. Sometimes they don't, at which time another board member needs to fulfill this role. One person I interviewed said they had a board member come to them once who declared that they are only on the board for the executive's spiritual uplifting. They called themselves this leader's "soul care" person.

As a last resort, if a board does not feel comfortable, they may want to form a triangular arrangement with someone, perhaps a pastor, who may be able to fill this role and report back to the board.

I interviewed a former board chair who I know did it right as it relates to a proper relationship with their executive. This person has been on multiple boards and also happens to be the solicitor (attorney) for many school districts. She handles difficult situations between school boards and the superintendents and staffs that run those public schools.

The relationship I focused on included the complete life of the executive and the intercession desired between board and executive. Below are her words as she described her interactions with the executive leader of their multimillion-dollar Christian nonprofit:

> *There is a sanctity in the relationship between a board chair and a CEO concerning personal issues that might begin to affect the job.*
>
> *Everything revealed during the conversations within that relationship does not have to be passed on to the board right away. They should be shared when there are going to be public ramifications, if the leader needs time off or is seeking additional mentorship or counsel that the board needs to know about. There are definitely reasons the board needs to know these things.*
>
> *It is not the weight of the chair to bear those personal responsibilities. However, this person, this leader, often stands alone.*
>
> *For instance, if a leader shares with a board chair that they have a child dealing with addiction issues they may tell the board there are family issues at home and this leader needs leave, or we are going to relax some of the requirements around work schedule. But the chair protects them personally. I may tell the board that I'm not going to get into specifics until the issues affect job performance and what the board is evaluating them on.*
>
> *I do think there is a level of protection that needs to exist there. Even in the Christian community, it is human nature that as soon as the board knows details, they will view the person differently. I don't think the average board member can separate it. Also, I, as the board chair, want them to be able to evaluate the leader strictly on their job performance. If the leader is able to maintain the stress of a family situation on one side and still perform, all*

is good. I think sometimes everyone knowing the personal issues in detail colors their actions (in the mind of the board member). For instance, every time they raise their voice, are in conflict with someone, or are late to work, everyone wonders if it was due to the personal situation.

This was the relationship between a particular board chair and CEO, but this relationship can be carried on by a board member or a third party.

A proper relationship between board and executive that allows for honesty and transparency in areas that may be personal, as well as organizational responsibilities, can be achieved. Keep in mind that this can only be done if self-examination and humility are part of the equation for both parties.

One founder and experienced board member I interviewed put it this way: "The leader has to know the board is 'for them.' The heart of the board has to be for that person as a human being and not just as a nonprofit executive."

It is the level of this support and genuine caring that determines where the line is in delving into an executive's personal life. This can determine the level of cooperation that will be exhibited. It is this level of genuine support that will promote transparency in a way that represses the threat of consequence.

I would also submit to you that the conscious pursuit of this type of relationship will carry throughout the organization and create a culture that will promote openness, creativity, and growth.

This type of relationship does not happen by coincidence or by chance. It is no different than a nonprofit coming out of the year in the black. Both take conscious effort and focus.

As with everything else in a nonprofit organization, the board is in control.

CHAPTER: 8

COMMUNITY: YES, YOU HAVE A ROLE

ONE OF the many people I interviewed for this book is a woman who founded an urban ministry that has grown quite successfully over their history and has impacted thousands. It was not easy, and people thought she was nuts. But she had a calling from God, and that was all she needed.

She recalled one time when she was struggling during the founding of the ministry, searching God's word for encouragement when no one else seemed to understand her plight. While reading her Bible nearly 20 years later, she came to a verse that encouraged her during that rough time. In the margin she found a note to God in response, "Yes, but please send me someone with skin on." She wasn't particular. She just wanted one person to talk to, to encourage her, to speak God's truth to her.

Everyone, including the executive leader, is accountable for their own life. The accountability structure that an executive sits under has a role in helping to prevent the fall of a nonprofit executive, as well as all of the traditional duties and responsibilities that come along with being a board of directors.

The people the executive leader needs to help them stay on track, including the desired "person with skin on," are found way beyond themselves and the board of directors.

In fact, there are people all around an executive leader who can impact their life much more than the formal structures around that leader. There are people and groups with access to the life of an executive that the board simply does not have. Certainly, family would be at the top of that list. But the list could include congregations, constituencies, community members, casual observers, friends, acquaintances, etc.

There are relationships around the executive that might be very new, without the hang-ups and judgments of past issues. There may be trusted relationships that have been built over many years that the leader leans on in times of trial. And then there are the casual relationships somewhere in-between.

Those people need to be activated, and they need to recognize that their impact on the leader can be paramount in the prevention of a leadership fall. Those relationships can rise above all other relationships for three reasons:

1. They are natural and more genuine because there is no professional structure or obligation, which allows for more openness and transparency.

2. Fear of retribution within the organization is typically shuttered.

3. The transparency and openness these informal relationships bring can reveal issues that may culminate in an executive fall earlier.

Of course, the sheer number of those people outside the formal structures is so much greater. As I have previously written, there can be a tremendous amount of pressure that can come from all of the people around the executive. That pressure, if not handled properly, can result in a fall.

Those groups of people can also bring an incredible volume of invaluable encouragement and wisdom.

Many times, when people see an executive struggling, we hear the phrase, "They really need to do something," meaning the accountability structure around the leader. What is forgotten is that we all have a responsibility for the support and encouragement of one another. "They" may actually be I or we.

Sometimes people outside the accountability structure need to perform a Courageous Ask.

I believe the responsibility we, as onlookers, feel must be elevated when it comes to Christian leaders who are serving us and the community while they strive to represent Christ on earth.

Very few of us are going to be the person who deals directly with whatever the struggle might be, although we could be and should desire to be.

I try to remember what author Nancy Duarte wrote, "Sometimes all it takes is a kind word of encouragement to get your heroes back on the right path."[32]

Well, I believe it takes a hero to do just that. You can be a hero by extending that kind word of encouragement that gets a nonprofit leader back on track.

HOW DO WE SEE OUR LEADERS?

Executives, whether they are pastors or nonprofit executives in our context, are put on a pedestal. It's not that the typical person necessarily believes they belong there or desires to put them there. But it is human nature that this happens.

The general public often places much higher expectations on leaders than they do on themselves. Sometimes it is appropriate, and the leader has put themselves in that position. In some cases, it is simply scriptural. For instance, James 3 points out that those who teach will be judged more strictly, thereby heightening the expectations of those who lead and teach.

But what about when we accept, and enact, those elevated expectations and forget the humanity of our leaders? Too many times a community heaps on a leader the expectation that they are to perform with the perfection of Jesus and not simply be a Jesus follower and disciple just like them, but with a unique calling and heightened responsibility.

Too many times when a leader shows human imperfection, the respect we have for them is damaged. Leaders fall under strict judgment, and we forget they are no less fallible than us. The imperfection they have colors any positive experience we would have had with them otherwise. While most of us acknowledge this strict, hypocritical judgment and recognize it as not being how we want to treat our leaders, it is a difficult battle to fight in our own attitudes and minds.

No matter who the leader is, they are not Jesus. But please allow me to reverently make some comparisons.

"Pretty blue eyes and curly brown hair and a clear complexion is how you see Him as He dies for your sins." Those are the words of Todd Agnew in his song "My Jesus."

Isn't this the Jesus we choose to see in our everyday life? I mean, don't we see the Jesus reaching out His hand to us, the Jesus holding a lamb, the Jesus guiding the hand of the surgeon as he performs surgery on a loved one, the Jesus holding a child, the Jesus teaching a crowd, or the picture of Jesus in all his perfectly manicured glory hanging on the cross with the bright light behind Him highlighting His silhouette? That's who we typically see, right?

The second part of the lyric from Todd Agnew's song provides a contrast to the beginning: "But the word says He was battered and scarred or did we miss that part." I think most people do. Absolutely brilliant lyrics.

What we have here in this song is an entirely accurate depiction of Jesus in our mind's eye no matter which view we choose to see Jesus from at a particular moment of time in our lives.

How do we see our leaders? Battered and scarred, accepting the unjust punishment of this world? Damaged? Perfect, with pretty blue eyes and curly brown hair? Or how about an embodiment of the perfect pictures as described in the previous paragraphs?

We may have an incredible amount of respect for our executive leaders. In fact, maybe it's admiration because they have so inspired us. This is especially true if they are founders who have seemingly created something from nothing with God's guidance. We may be amazed at what God has done through them to courageously move forward in accomplishing what people thought was impossible. We hold them in high esteem and put them on a pedestal.

Somewhere inside us, we recognize they are human and are not perfect, but our focus remains on the great things they have done. We forget their humanness since they have been able to put on airs that everything is under control for the benefit of the advancement of the organization.

Somehow Jesus supernaturally handled all that was thrown at Him and responded in a way that only He could; He was God incarnate.

He responded with incredible grace and mercy to those who were the true offenders.

I suspect that many times we expect our leaders to be Jesus Himself instead of a fallible human being—a follower and disciple just like us. But they are not Jesus.

I hope that makes you think a bit.

While I know I am using Jesus to compare and contrast the picture of our nonprofit executives, the same principles apply in a non-Christian organization.

Part of the proactive approach to preventing the fall of a nonprofit leader is recognizing they are no different than us and properly applying that recognition.

PUT IT IN PRACTICE

Todd Agnew in his song says that he thinks that "Jesus would prefer Beale Street to the stained glass crowd." I agree.

Setting aside the fact that I enjoy Beale Street in Memphis (love that barbecue!), I believe what Todd is saying is that Jesus preferred to be in the real world where people are living real life, experiencing real joy in between the very real battles of the hurt, pain, and other difficulties that infect their lives.

Hurt, pain, and difficulty are ever present in the life of a nonprofit executive leader. In his book *Leadership Pain*, Samuel Chand says that leadership is actually a magnet for pain and comes in many forms. Leadership pain is part of the real world Jesus would prefer to be present in. While many people in the Christian community strive to represent Jesus in the real world, they forget that they can represent Jesus in the life of an executive nonprofit leader who is dealing with very real leadership pain.

Does the real world exist in your church or nonprofit? More specifically, is the real world allowed to exist in your church or nonprofit?

Another line in Agnew's song says, "My Jesus would never be accepted in my church. The blood and dirt on His feet might stain the carpet." This is a picture of society coming into our Christian communities and our acceptance of it. Don't we want broken society coming into our churches?

Sometimes that society comes in the form of our leader who is struggling in a church or nonprofit.

I certainly recognize what James 4:4 states: "Don't you know that friendship with the world means enmity against God?" But there must be room for the grace and mercy that the Gospel provides.

I'm not talking about friendship with the world; I am talking about proper application of grace and mercy to the world that needs the message we have to offer. That is sometimes hard as we battle our own human pride.

I have seen tremendous grace and mercy toward the sinner provided in a wide variety of Christian contexts. But I have also seen and experienced the opposite, when a leader sinfully brings the real world into the Christian community. A real world that everyone, including Christians, exists in and that God addresses all throughout scripture.

Are the people that brought the real world in still genuinely loved and accepted without harsh judgment and arrogance, as if we don't fight some of the same battles, only secretly?

Yes, I understand the need for appropriate action to take place in the unrepentant heart of a sinner in a church or nonprofit context. That is certainly described in this book. The board has a responsibility to deal with this type of thing.

Here is a good question: is your leader, whether a pastor or the executive of a Christian nonprofit, allowed to be part of the fallible real world, and are they still loved and accepted if they knowingly or unknowingly allow the real world into their own life?

The inability of a Christian nonprofit leader to be themselves, and to live with the fear of transparency with their accountability structures or those they come in contact with can be the source of a fall. This fear can definitely cause the loneliness and isolation that may lead to a fall.

And what are they afraid of? They are afraid that people will see that they are no different than them. That's a very real fear, but a fear that should not exist.

I hope you choose to be where Jesus chooses to be, walking alongside real people (including our leaders) in the real world.

YOU, YES, YOU!

I'm sure you've found yourself praying for someone to enter into the life of a loved one and say or do just the right thing to help that loved one jump back on the right track or even help them find the track.

Why do people choose to pray on someone else's behalf? Of course, scripture tells us to pray for one another. A person might have been praying for someone, but let's be honest, many times they pray that the struggling leader will listen to them. That hasn't worked.

There are two paths a person typically has taken prior to backing off and solely interceding through prayer for a struggling leader:

1.   They have tried to help them, and all advice has been pushed aside. Usually this person has tried and tried, sometimes even nagged the leader. The leader has built a wall in their mind based on recent attempts of manipulation or other challenges in the relationship. In seeing the wall, the person now praying

has given up.

2.   The person has determined that they are not the person to approach the leader. This could be human fear, but it could be simple wisdom in knowing the situational context, relationships, and any number of other reasons.

No matter who you are in the life of a leader outside their formal accountability structure—friend, neighbor, staff member, constituent, donor, congregant, or even casual acquaintance—you just might be the answer to someone's hopes or prayers in the life of a leader. You may be part of the proactive approach in preventing a leadership fall and not even know it.

Many times what a floundering leader needs is an objective person who is separate from family and the accountability structure. These are the places where walls unfortunately get built in the leader's life.

In fact, while the leader is ultimately accountable for themselves, these two groups—family and accountability structure—may even help build the wall between the Christian nonprofit executive and God.

It's very hard for board members and family who love the leader they see falling to stop doing things like sending scripture verses and videos they think might inspire and make the difference. They want to help fix them, and for the leader to see the clear path that they see.

In the possibly deluded mind of the leader, these types of things may make them resentful toward the sender, and as a by-product that resentment may carry on to God.

This is a great example of when a person in the community might be able to make the difference in the life of a struggling leader, whether they are falling or not.

You may be the answer to someone's prayer in the life of a loved one,

Christian leader, or executive. You may be the one that provides the friendship that prevents a leadership fall.

FRIENDSHIP

In a 2016 statistical update on pastors, Churchleadership.org wrote that 58 percent of pastors stated they do not have any good, true friends. They also reported that 27 percent of pastors stated they have no one to turn to if they are facing a crisis.[33]

In my experience, these statistics easily convert to all forms of Christian nonprofit leaders.

It's difficult for pastors to have friends in their home community. When asked, many will say their best friends are out of town, usually a friend from seminary.

My interviews and research reveal a main reason: people are generally uncomfortable affording friendship to a pastor and many Christian leaders.

A former pastor who now is the CEO of a Christian nonprofit said, "I have five or six people locally who I speak to honestly, and pretty transparently, and each gets a part of who I am (a part of my life)." He continued, "But no one has the whole, full picture." He said that it is a problem, but claimed that it is okay. Is it?

When I followed up with this executive and pastor and asked them why people only get pieces, they pointed out that most of the friends they referred to are leaders themselves. This executive said that time did not permit deep friendship, since the time they typically talk is at functions or within another agenda.

That is simply not good enough in being proactive to prevent a fall.

I broached this topic with the CEO of a million-dollar Christian nonprofit and their answer was this: "The people you become closest to are your biggest funders or people engaged in the mission in some capacity."

This creates quite the conflict when the people you are closest to are also people that can adversely affect the nonprofit if they don't like something you do, or see you struggling as you open up to them.

It's been said that in order to have a friend, you need to be a friend. I ask you: aren't pastors and Christian leaders friends to a lot of people? It doesn't seem that the statement applies to Christian leaders since 58 percent of pastors do not have one good, true friend. Where are the reciprocal relationships they need like everyone else?

One long-term pastor I interviewed said that they "never really had a close friend, but yet I am always expected to befriend everyone."

Another pastor I interviewed gave this example from their experience: "People we know mention they are having a Fourth of July picnic, but neglect to invite us." They continued, "Nobody wants a preacher there because that changes the type of conversation they can have."

That really hits the crux of it, doesn't it?

Joe Jensen, a former pastor who now works as director of strategic partnerships and church engagement at Barna Group, says, "Your pastor is more than your church leader, he or she is also your brother or sister, a fallible human being in need of the same mercy, compassion, companionship, and encouragement as you."[34]

People need people. Leaders need people. Pastors and Christian leaders need you as true friends.

It's much easier to reach out to someone who needs you than to reach out to someone when you need them. I can assure you that Christian leaders need people to reach out to them.

Andy Vaughn wrote, "My grandparents had a ministry that basically went something like this: Get to know their pastor, and then be their friend. That's it. They understood the drain and strain it was to constantly be 'on.' Always being the leader, the guide, the one with all the answers is not only tiring, but it's also unhealthy. Pastors need friends to laugh with, to cry with, and to help counsel them along their own spiritual journey."[35]

Pastors and Christian leaders have the same desire "to be human together" as anyone else does.

People reaching out to Christian leaders, putting aside any discomfort and insecurity they may have, and creating friendships just might be the key in preventing the fall of that leader.

COMMUNITY EXPECTATIONS

Nonprofit executives, including pastors, are on the public dole. Primarily, the support that sustains the mission they are so passionate about, and their paycheck, comes from the public in one way or another. That support ultimately comes from individuals, foundations, and publicly supported government agencies among other sources. There are many self-sustaining, fee-for-service nonprofits out there, but by and large, nonprofits rely on the public.

There's a propensity for Christian nonprofit executives to be taken for granted, even taken advantage of. I heard this loud and clear during my interviews. For the most part, this frustration seemed to come from leaders who struggled to draw boundaries because of their big hearts and their innate, self-imposed responsibility to those who support them.

Christian leaders, especially pastors, many times feel disrespected. Those inside the accountability structures can help with this, but those outside those structures can especially help with this as they are sensitive to the limitations of their leader.

Pastors described the many ways a congregation expects that all of the pastor's time is actually their time, and tend to treat it as such.

"People will do to their ministers what they wouldn't do to their doctors," one pastor told me. "People stop into the office and say, 'Hey, pastor, you busy?' What am I going to say, even though I have a pen in my hand and papers all over my desk? Even my dog needs an appointment at the veterinarian."

Now, this particular pastor was sure to acknowledge the pastoral duty inherent in their vocation and was gracious in their descriptions, but I could also sense their frustration.

"We want to be a certain person, but in reality when we don't feel respected, or we feel taken for granted, that humanness comes in and frustrates us," the pastor added.

I remember so many times as a nonprofit executive that I stopped into the office of a colleague because I was in the neighborhood. I have even done this to pastors myself. Such disrespect.

What about meetings? Many times the community expects a nonprofit executive to be in every meeting imaginable.

As a Christian free clinic CEO, people expected me to be on every committee related to healthcare and every committee related to Christian causes in the community. Put those things together and my life became meetings. As I was working to build the clinic, I faced internal pressure and external expectations—people were visibly disappointed when I didn't participate in their causes. That is hard to navigate for the nonprofit executive.

One study I read on Pastoralcareinc.com revealed that 75 percent of pastors report spending four to five hours per week in needless meetings. The same report said that 72 percent of pastors report working between 55 and 75 hours per week.[36]

Nonprofit consultant and writer Joan Gerry wrote in *Harvard Business*

Review, "Your jaw would drop if you knew how many executive directors work 65 hours a week and are paid for 20."[37]

Those four to five hours could have been spent with family or doing something else to keep them sane.

The expectations of the community around nonprofit executives need to change. It won't be easy. As a community, we need to find strategies to ease their legitimate frustrations and burdens. The community also needs to understand that it is difficult for a nonprofit executive to set boundaries and needs to be accepting when they do.

We need to consider them as professionals, making appointments even though they say it's okay not to. We need to ease the expectation that they are to be at the church every time the doors are open. We need to take leadership in our committees to ease the pressure on our leaders.

In short, we must "do to others what you would have them do to you," the golden rule found in Matthew 7:12.

A SIDENOTE ABOUT THE BOARD FOR THE COMMUNITY

There are many great reasons to become a board member, but there are also drawbacks. Many board members are volunteers, and they do their best to make wise decisions representing the entity. They must have a courage of purpose to stand up, even within themselves, to the critical nature of those they are serving. (Sometimes this even includes fellow board members.)

I remember one such case that I experienced. My wife and I had been attending the same church for almost 20 years. A new pastor came in, and I loved his messages.

But there were other issues that formed a problem for me in this pastor's life. I was not on a board or accountability structure but was involved in many church ministries. I tried to get to know this pastor. It was not easy, as the issues I saw made it difficult. I was someone who became alienated by him.

I was forced to trust the leadership and the board to do what they thought was wise, while I prayed and tried to stay positive and encouraging.

But as the board failed to act, my wife and I reluctantly, after much prayer and reflection, decided to move on and find another church to attend.

A few years later the pastor announced he was leaving the church. When the pastor announced this, church members, including staff, started coming forward with stories of mistreatment and other problems. This put the board in a tough spot. Do they let him ride out his several-months' notice or ask him to leave? The board chose to ask him to leave and paid him severance.

Of course, there are tons of details that are really not relevant to my point. Unfortunately, this situation is too common in the Church.

As an experienced board member and leader, and knowing many of the current board members, I knew the board was falling under heavy scrutiny while doing its best to weigh all information and make their best decision while seeking God's wisdom through study and prayer. There was tremendous pressure on these servants, and I knew them to be solid Christian men.

The next Sunday we chose to attend that church and I searched out each board member I could find. I did this for weeks. I shared words of encouragement while not picking a side, and shared how much they individually had impacted me.

Some of them broke down in tears, and I saw the eyes of others well up. As you would expect, some were tough guys and just said, "Thank you," fearing the show of emotion. But each of them was starving for people to encourage them, people outside their direct sphere of influence who had no obligation to build them up.

It made a big difference to them that we came back, out of the blue, to show them support. After the impact they had on me in my Christian growth, directly or indirectly, I finally had the opportunity to pay them back.

The average person has quite the influence on an organization, and that influence many times is through the board. While boards desire and need our input, we need to be sure we are an encouragement to them and share with them all of the great work we see them doing, as well as sharing the opportunities we see.

If you are reading this book and don't find yourself in a position of leadership or authority, that does not mean you don't have the opportunity to lift up executive leadership and help carry some of their burden. Have courage to do so. You could be the difference between a leader taking the wrong path of despair or moving forward in confident hope of a better day. You may be proactive at exactly the right time and have a significant impact.

You may think you are just the average Joe Shmoe to your leader. But your genuine encouragement and action will not be average to your leader.

Muster the humility and courage to lift up leaders! They need you.

Remember, "Sometimes all it takes is a kind word of encouragement to get your heroes back on the right path."

CHAPTER 9

REPAIR, RECONCILE, RESTORE:
RISE AGAIN AFTER THE FALL

*W*HY DO *leaders who fall not expect consequences?*

Why does it seem like they blame everyone else? They hurt a ton of people and have damaged relationships beyond repair, yet they try to minimize it.

They expect to be able to snap their fingers and watch everything instantly go back to the way it used to be. They like to throw around concepts and words like forgiveness, mercy, and grace. But, through their actions they have hurt people to their core, perhaps irreparably damaging the people and organizations they represent.

Why is the pressure put on everyone else to forgive and move on just because the person who fell changed their direction?

I am so angry that they just expect us, expect me, to push this aside. They have a lot more to prove than to simply come out and proclaim, "I have changed." They are so selfish!

These are some of the natural reactions that occur all around a fallen leader. The feelings and thoughts are humanly legit, make no mistake about it. They are especially legit when the fallen leader has experienced strong conviction and desires to change direction among all of the upheaval they have caused.

But they have betrayed people and destroyed trust. They have driven people to their breaking point. That does not get repaired at the snap of the fingers and deserves its own measure of grace and mercy from the fallen leader.

It requires time. It requires patience. It requires a supernatural effort that can only be orchestrated by the leader surrendering themselves to God and His direction.

I have personally walked through this in my own life and in the lives of those around me. I have also walked through this with other fallen leaders and those around them. And I have observed all of this from a distance as a hurt public looks on fallen national leaders.

I do not want any misunderstanding as you read the following pages that talk about the reactions all around a leader after they have fallen.

The leader is fully accountable. The fallen leader sometimes comes out of a fall still deluded. The fallen leader, sometimes in their continued delusion, can be insensitive to those around them. The fallen leader most times has no clue how much damage they have done.

Frankly, much of this describes me after my fall. But I have watched this same thing occur as a pattern many times in the lives of others.

So, as you read the following pages in this chapter, please remember these acknowledgments. I am a person looking back at the world I lived in as if looking through Alice's looking glass. It seems so distant.

Because this book is focused on a proactive approach before the fall, this chapter seeks to touch on the period after a fall occurs and is not exhaustive.

REACTIONS AFTER THE FALL

My family reacted to the revelations concerning my fall with horror, as was appropriate and as would have been expected. It sent us down an extremely difficult road, and eventually I filed for divorce as I battled my own demons. While we did come back together, it was a years-long struggle that will have lifelong consequences.

How did the community, especially the Christian community, react to my fall?

At first, they were surprised. Their surprise quickly moved to disappointment, anger, and disgust. People say all the time that they recognize leaders aren't perfect, but I have experienced that when they show themselves as not being perfect, many of those same people act surprised. After the initial surprise, people seemed to break into four groups:

1. The legalists who genuinely think that after you give your life to Christ you lose all desire and ability to be a fallen human, even though they, too, have their struggles. This is a very well-meaning group. After expressing their disgust and disappointment that I didn't meet their expectations (which had very little to do with Jesus's expectations), they would either not talk to me anymore or they would continually send me scripture verses and videos as if one of those would somehow "fix" me. But one thing they were not willing to do, without their own personal agenda, was to get down in the mud with me and help me walk through my personal struggle. This group pretty much lost access to me, and I cut them out of my life.

2. There was a group I had to actually convince that I did something wrong. I call them the justifiers. This group really cared about me and wanted to help. Keep in mind that this was a three-month emotional affair that never turned physical.

For some, this formed the line of moral failure and took the situation beyond their understanding. I would sit across the table from them trying to convince them I did something wrong, often to no avail. Many times they could come to a point where they accepted that I should not have done what I did, but they thought it was no big deal. They wondered why the clinic was involved in my personal matters. This group I allowed skeptically in my life.

3.   There was a group of people who said nothing with their mouths, but said everything with their eyes and actions. I call them the quiet skeptics. This was the group that kept me guessing as I wondered what they were thinking. Considering the position I was in, my assumptions were almost always negative. This group would avoid me, and on the occasion that our eyes would meet, they would give me what I perceived as an unpleasant look, or they would look away. This group was an excellent group of supporters and acquaintances before the fall, but disappeared when the fall happened. Much of my board falls into this group, especially after I was fired and even to this day.

4.   The fourth group, the wise counselors, continually reminded me lovingly who I was in Christ. They never let me make excuses for my actions and shared videos and scripture that would encourage me in a way that Christ himself would. The actions taken by the fourth group are in some cases the same as the others, but clearly came with a different heart, a heart that was focused on reconciliation and restoration, not their own personal agenda. They got down in the mud, listened to me (held their tongues many times I'm sure), displayed patience, allowed me to cry, and walked me back to Him. This group had the most access to me because of their Christ-like love of a sinner like me. Their Courageous Ask was much appreciated because of their sincerity. Praise God for the fourth group!

Unfortunately, most people fell into the first group directly after the fall, right or wrong, I found myself building bitterness against the Church, not God, because of how I was treated by those around me who were proclaimed Christians. In fact, many times those who lived a more secular life provided more profitable compassion, love, and guidance.

I had one fallen leader tell me that, "People didn't want their name associated with me. When people saw that my perceived influence in the community had diminished, they didn't want anything to do with me."

This was definitely my experience, and I lived the cliché, "Christians shoot their wounded."

I am so thankful for the fourth group who, even though their numbers were much smaller, had the biggest impact on me.

For the person around the fallen leader, the big question you'll face internally is this: who are you committed to being if you are close to a leader who has fallen? It is best to make that choice before there is a fall around you.

It will take an almost supernatural effort to stay focused, control emotions, and consciously love if you choose to follow through as a committed member of the fourth group. It is not likely you can do it alone, as prayer and help from others is vital.

REACTIONS AFTER THE FALL: GOING TOO FAR

The weeks and months after my fall were very difficult and emotional for everyone involved—my wife and family, extended family, the board and organization, the community, and me.

I am so thankful that God helped my wife and I through the toughest time in our marriage and most things are repaired in our relationship. God is so gracious!

But there are still challenges hanging on as long-term consequences. We both agree that many times things were taken too far, and that is the reason we have many of the long-term consequences. We look back and see all of the emotional reactions that took place that created permanent damage that did not have to happen.

Sometimes the reaction to the fall, and the collateral damage caused by that reaction, reaches a destructive level nearly equal to the offense itself. If this happens, there may be so much destruction that no one will be able to make it back to the path.

This reminds me of the story of a friend of mine and his wife when they purchased a home that needed some work. Honestly, the house was livable but needed to be gutted.

They were so excited about the possibilities.

Instead of moving into the house and working on it room by room, they early on got swept up in the emotion of dreaming and destruction. They went from room to room gutting the place.

As they entered the last few areas needing renovation, they started to experience a feeling that overwhelmed them.

They became demoralized by what it would take to repair all of the damage. Discouragement settled in right next to the overwhelmed feeling. They started to question what they had done.

It felt pretty good and brought short-term satisfaction as they were doing it, but now what should they do? Was too much damage done? Could they recover? Did they want to recover? There was no doubt that the house would be beautiful in the end, but did they want to go through the many months of sacrifice and work to make it what they dreamed of?

In the end they decided they went too far. They did not want to commit the next year or so to the reconstruction of the house, even if it would end up being their dream home. They felt defeated and sold the house.

Like my friend's house, the ability to restore a fallen leader to the body is often dependent on how much damage was done at the outset of the revelation of the fall. Many times our reaction to the fall, because of legitimate feelings and emotions, causes so much damage it is very difficult to see a pathway to restoration.

Examples of collateral damage that I have seen go too far unnecessarily in the emotional early stages after a leadership fall include familial relationship damage, financial ruin, physical damage, and organizational destruction.

We sometimes allow a bitter root to develop that is so deep we cannot kill it. As time goes by, we may even recognize, through clearer thinking, what God would want us to do. Sometimes our pride, embarrassment, or some other stumbling block keeps us discouraged in a way that doesn't allow us to rebuild.

And this is where some executives and those around them give up.

But if they give up, there is possibly tremendous potential not yet seen that might not be realized.

Of course, there will be emotion at first. But, as quickly as possible, God-centered priorities need to be established in order to control the expanse of collateral damage that may prevent the quickest recovery possible for the organization and the leader.

This is such hard stuff! It will test those around the leader to their core— to the very core of their faith, to the very core of their identity, to the very core of their loyalties.

At the outset of the offense, those closest to it find it most difficult to see beyond the hurt.

REACTIONS AFTER THE FALL:
BUT THEY DID THIS TO ME!

The leader did do it to you! Most times numerous people will feel this personalization of the fall at various levels. It's only natural.

The depth of the hurt is usually directly proportional to how close a person is to the actual fall.

"Moral failure" has its own unique level of pain and hurt to those closest to the fall. Unfortunately, this is the most common of executive falls.

Human pain lurks around every corner. There are triggers everywhere. Scenarios never stop playing. Sleep is sparse, and exhaustion sets in.

The hurt could be so traumatic that a person may be permanently changed. Every thought or action that a person close to the fall encounters is somehow related to the devastation of the fall. Those closest to a fall can become another person. They cannot see past their hurt and want the offender to hurt as much as they have been hurt.

There is a constant quest for information, and when it is not available, assumptions are made. The land of assumption is wrought with damage waiting to happen.

This is where the people not so close to the fall come in. These people might just be the most important part of the recovery because they can help with wise, levelheaded control of collateral damage.

Those on the periphery can help those closest to the fall see beyond their hurt and pain. They can remind them of who they are, helping them not allow bitterness to take root. Again, once it goes too far, it's hard to recover. People need people. Seems like I've heard that before...

THE POST-FALL ROLE OF THE LEADER:
THE HARD TRUTH

Fallen leader, it hurts. And it's hard to shake that hurt. It doesn't matter if what happened was self-inflicted or inflicted by others, or at what ratio, it hurts. You have risked the deepest part of your soul and laid your life out there for all to see, and something went awry. The same sets of eyes that looked on you with admiration during your high point now seem to look at you with disgust in your low point. Paranoia sets in. Not only are you feeling all eyes upon you and what happened, but the disappointment in yourself is unbearable.

What you are feeling is real—hopelessness, despair, disappointment, shame, loneliness, and uselessness. You are crushed. Your thoughts are confused, and you can't think straight.

All of this makes you want to run away, to pack everything up and go.

There is one question that every Christian leader who has taken a fall needs to ask, and quickly: How long until I give up? The answer to that question is the way out. You will eventually give up and surrender. How long it takes will determine the amount of collateral damage, how much damage to yourself is inflicted, and how long it will take everyone to recover, including yourself.

How long are you going to defend what happened and try to make people understand why it happened? How long are you going to keep giving yourself a pass on what happened, even if you don't express it openly?

The answers to all of these questions determine the amount of torment you are going to live with. For me, the daily torment was multiplied when I laid my head on the pillow at night. The torment did not stop until I got to the end of myself and tapped into God's supernatural power. I had to get out of my own way.

You are the offender in the eyes of those you have hurt and need to be held to account. But, fallen leader, you have a unique role to play when it comes to their true forgiveness of you. Ultimately, it is between them and God, but you can help.

The easiest thing for you to do, but the least profitable, is to sit back and blame them for their unforgiving spirit. The fact is, the choice you are making to not forgive them is one of the causes of torment I described earlier.

This book has been written with the humanness of the leader at the forefront. Well, now it is time for you to take that same grace and mercy that you expect from everyone else and apply it back to them. They are no more perfect than you are.

All throughout the book, especially in Chapter 6, I have talked about individual accountability. Well, now it is time to focus on God and your accountability to Him. Let me remind you: He loves you. He desires to forgive you. He has boundless grace and mercy for you. He knew the whole time you were going to do what you did and loved you anyway, no different than the trials of many biblical heroes like David and Peter. Now it's time to turn to Him. It's time to stop focusing on those around you and focus on your relationship with God.

I have lived through this fire, and I know it's ugly.

That's the hard truth. You can choose individual accountability. You can choose to give up your pride and protection of self. You can choose to follow God's way. You can choose to draw a line and stop the collateral damage. You can choose reconciliation and restoration. But you must choose.

There is a light at the end of the tunnel. There is a Promised Land. There is plenty of room for encouragement.

Pastor Rick Warren said, "Other people are going to find healing in your wounds. Your greatest life messages and your most effective ministry will come out of your deepest hurts."

You can do it. But first you must choose.

THE POST-FALL ROLE OF THE LEADER: A PROPER ADJUSTMENT

Who doesn't love Walt Disney World? Okay, maybe that all-day battle with the bad wheel of a stroller on a 95-degree day with high humidity and ice cream running down the arms and face of your child wasn't your favorite moment.

But dreams do come true there.

In central Florida you can find snow. Yes, snow! You can regularly find the fake stuff during Mickey's Very Merry Christmas Party on Main Street, U.S.A.

Believe it or not, it actually has naturally snowed at Walt Disney World.

This reminds me of a story I read by Robert Niles, the founder and editor of *Theme Park Insider*:

> *Even in December, the weather in Central Florida remains pleasant most days. But about once per decade or so, a nasty cold front penetrates the state, freezing orange trees, tourists, and even residents. The morning of December 23, 1989, brought one of those fronts. My shift that day was to open at Tom Sawyer Island.*

During his shift it became clear that the park was going to have to close as the fog was very thick and the roller coasters could not operate on frozen tracks. He continues:

> *Lake Buena Vista, we've got a problem.*

On my way over to the tunnels to change clothes and clock out, I felt something fly into my eye. I blinked, instinctively, and brought my hand to my eye to wipe away whatever it was. But I felt the offending speck melt to water instead. Standing in the middle of Frontierland, I looked to the sky and saw…snowflakes.

It was snowing…at Walt Disney World.[38]

That's not the only time it snowed at Walt Disney World. The *Orlando Sentinel* says that the first recorded snow in Orlando was in 1977.

Magic at Walt Disney World. But it just does not snow in Orlando, agreed? Yet both of these times it did.

So how do you think Walt Disney World reacted to the snow?

Do you think they brought in rail cars full of snow-melting salt to stockpile? Did they go out and purchase snowplows capable of clearing the lots just in case it happened again? Did they add a parka to the required uniform? Did they draw up emergency plans and build snow shelters for their guests to prepare for the storms that were sure to come again?

I doubt they did any of this. I'm sure they recognized the snow for what it was, an anomaly.

Now, it's up to you to decide if the cause of your fall was an anomaly. I'm sure we all want to say that yes, it was. But really, was it?

This is where you need to engage others in order to properly examine what happened. We are our number one fan and can justify anything. If we are truly sincere about identification of the root cause, we need to be humble and ask for the guidance of those wise individuals around us who are willing and able to walk the journey with us.

If it was an anomaly, okay. There is no sense in buying snowplows and ice melt and throwing everyone into a frenzy.

That does not mean there are not actions to be taken and you drop it, expecting everyone around you to drop it as well. Yes, it was out of the ordinary and not part of who you are, but this anomaly most likely hurt people, and you have some work to do.

If it was not and has a consistent sinful root, that's a different story. Then you need to dig in.

In my case I really needed to get back in touch with my identity in Christ. I had allowed my identity to be stolen away from me. Satan was the thief whom I allowed to work through other people and through my weakness. I became deluded, and I was living in a fantasyland. For me, it was not an anomaly and had much deeper roots that I needed to deal with, roots that I am still dealing with today.

You see, in forming the clinic, I was fighting for "the least of these" and became well known. Soon, the identity I had became puffed up and started to yield to the public persona. That desire to be puffed up eased the insecurities I had developed over many years. It was this insecurity that formed the root that took away my ability to call my fall an anomaly.

After giving my identity over to the public nonprofit identity, the other identity faded, and I fell. Everything changed. If I wanted to regain the identity I lost, then I needed to get real about who I was, who I had become. It was not pretty. And the fall was no anomaly.

Leader, if you have fallen, was it an anomaly? If it was, deal with it. If it wasn't, deal with it. Either way, it is time to find humility and bring others into the battle with you for a proper adjustment.

THE POST-FALL ROLE OF THE ACCOUNTABILITY STRUCTURE: THE DIFFICULT DECISION

A leader's fall puts the organization's board members in a difficult position. As a board member, you are hurt, probably feeling betrayed.

You may even be mad. You have to protect the organization.

But there is a part of you that feels compassion for the fallen leader as their world crashes down around them.

How do you prioritize your roles—Christian individual with a duty to God, board member with fiduciary responsibilities to protect the entity, community member and influencer, provider of services? And all of that is on top of running your own life with your own family.

How do you do that? There is no one answer or set of answers because all situations are different.

What I will do, though, is recommend 10 principles for the Christian nonprofit board to follow in dealing with a fallen leader that come from my own experience, from conducted interviews, and from research. Other than the first two, the rest are in no particular order.

1. Your ultimate responsibility, way above being the entity, is your relationship with God. There will never be a time that you are not ultimately accountable to God. This is very important to realize as people try to pressure you into taking their position and play on your emotions. This could be other board members, the community, the fallen leader, family, etc. It's important to keep the centerline on God and scripture, maintaining the courage and integrity that make you a solid board member.

2. Protect God in the community. I'm not so arrogant as to think God really needs your protection. But what God does desire is for you to be His hands, His feet, and His mouthpiece—His representative at the board table and in the community. It's possible that the leader needs to be removed from their position or that difficult decisions will need to be made, but how you react and how a fallen leader is treated is what the community will see. There are instances where the aftermath of a fall creates a much

worse impression of the Church than the fall itself. For their part, the board needs to do their best to represent God well.

3. The fallen leader is still valuable. They messed up in a big way and hurt a lot of people. That does not mean they do not have value. One thing I have been told, and experienced, is that the board disappears from the life of a fallen leader after final decisions are made, portraying indifference. If everyone treats the fallen Christian nonprofit leader as if they have no value, at least in the eyes of Christ, they may start to believe it themselves. This may launch them into a place of despair that is hard to recover from in a lifetime. The board must do what the board must do as the entity. But everyone, the board and the offender, is a fallible human being and that must not be forgotten. This must go beyond words.

4. Author and speaker Kay Warren said, "Broken trees can still bear fruit." Recognize that this is hopefully a short-term issue in the life of the fallen executive. It especially is short term in the light of eternity. The board doesn't want to be the stumbling block that causes long-term disarray in the life of the fallen executive that is trying to recover. For instance, after possible recovery the leader will need to find employment. They will still have a full life to live. The board should attempt to be a help, as deemed appropriate considering the circumstance, in the recovery of their entire life and not just this relatively short-term circumstance. One board chair I interviewed who led the board in terminating their fallen executive said, "Nothing should prevent the recovery of the leader." They continued, "A board needs to take the leader's heart into consideration and make tools available for the fallen leader to recover."

5. Make the wisest decision possible. Prayer and meditation are a must. Make decisions slowly and with all of the facts possible. Go with what you know and not with what you

assume. Reject any and all gossip that cannot be proven. Bring in a third party to investigate if possible, in order to prevent emotion and fear from guiding the process.

6. Do not yield to fear or public pressure. This happens way too often. Boards are left asking, "What will the donors think, and how will this affect our funding? Will the public lose faith in us as an organization? What if this hits social media? What does it say about me/us if we don't make a quick decisive decision?" Fear is a big human motivator. Public pressure many times drives this fear, especially in a Christian environment where the expectations of leadership, executives, and boards are much higher. In most situations, when a Christian leader falls, the public scrutiny will be short-lived if the accountability structure is focused, with conviction, on doing things to the best of their human ability God's way. This will translate to grace from most of the Christian community.

7. Love unconditionally. Yes, justice is important and must be enacted if needed. But recognize that accountability and church discipline, even in a nonprofit, are humanly easier than unconditional love. In other words, make decisions the hard way, not the easy way.

8. Search for facts without browbeating. It is not necessary to continually remind the leader of their mistakes after they have acknowledged them. No piling on. Use Jesus as an example. The woman caught in adultery and the woman at the well come to mind. Everyone knew the sins of the offenders, but He did not have to beat them into the ground with them. There is an appropriate level of reminder, but taking it too far is driving the fallen leader into a place they may not recover from.

9. Encourage communal care for the fallen leader. Because of

their position, a board may not be able to initially connect with the fallen leader. They should encourage others to reach out to them to help with the recovery.

10. Finally, grace is not a natural concept. Seek it. Fight for it. Allow it. Remember, you need it as well.

There is nothing that I am aware of in the life of a nonprofit board that is more difficult than the decisions that need to be made when a Christian executive falls for whatever reason. From my experience, it is heart wrenching.

The board's A#1 priority, beyond their duties to God, is the preservation and protection of the entity. A very close second is the reconciliation and restoration of the fallen leader.

THE POST-FALL ROLE OF THE COMMUNITY: HARD QUESTION, HARD ANSWER

After the initial shock and inevitable emotional reaction, is the basic focus of those around the fallen leader dependent on the post-fall actions of that fallen leader?

The hard answer to that hard question, especially for Christians, is no. The focus of everyone around a fallen leader is not dependent on the post-fall actions of the leader.

That's a hard pill to swallow for some. Remember, I said that the answer to the question lies in where the *focus* of those around a fallen leader is. This focus will drive the community reaction.

The fallen leader may still be in fantasyland (Christians call this delusion) and not be to a point that they recognize the full gravity of what they have done. They may even be antagonistic toward those who are trying to help them. Arrogance may be king.

The other possibility is that they may be completely broken in recognition of what they did. Their whole mind and their actions may revolve around making things right.

They may show genuine heartbreak in their actions.

After the initial shock and emotional outpouring, no matter how that may manifest, the answer solely lies in the focus of each individual around the leader.

Where do they want this to end up?

Some choose bitterness and anger. Some choose to focus on the fallen leader getting what they deserve. Some choose to make sure the leader hurts like they have been hurt. But some choose a different path.

The person that chooses the Christian path will focus on their own personal relationship with God and the restoration of the fallen leader to the family.

Now, specific actions to be taken by those around a fallen leader do differ by the severity of the fall and the way that fallen leader acts after the fall. That is true. But the primary focus needs to remain on reconciliation, restoration, and just plain love. Those three principled qualities can be shown no matter the actions of the fallen leader. But they may take some time.

Can that be done? It can, with caution. But it can be tricky.

In order to repair the circumstances that come with a fall, the individual, the organization, and the community need to proceed with great humility. And guess what? If one of the three decides to not move forward in humility, the others are not off the hook. Humility must be maintained.

In his book *Humility: True Greatness*, C. J. Mahaney defines humility as "honestly assessing ourselves in light of God's holiness and our sinfulness."

I really like that definition. It puts the standard where the standard should be and doesn't play games. The standard is in the Gospel and in scripture, not where current societal norms lie.

This is where we sometimes get stuck and find ourselves comparing and justifying.

Humility is vital, no matter who you are around the leader or if you are the leader yourself, to the positive long-term reconciliation and restoration of relationships.

Yes, the leader's actions can make it easier (a relative term) on those around them, but they may not choose or have the ability to make the right choices.

But, those around them often can.

THE POST-FALL ROLE OF THE COMMUNITY: INDIVIDUAL PRESENCE

A leader who has fallen learns quickly who their true friends are. As was indicated earlier about the leader who was at the highest level of public recognition before his fall, most people he thought were friends disappeared into thin air. "They didn't want their name associated with me," he said.

So, the question is, "Why?"

Most people around the fallen leader have no idea what to say. They are afraid they will get into an uncomfortable conversation with the fallen leader. The fear is that the leader did something that does not fly, and they will try to justify their actions to get them on their side to support something they just cannot, which will cause even greater conflict and lead to great discomfort.

I might suggest that they are possibly correct, as getting into a conversation about the situation might not be the best course. But that does not relieve you of your responsibility to God and the leader. What that leader is looking for at that moment, even if they are still deluded, is your presence.

That presence can be a physical presence or a presence of mind. An example of this physical presence without obligation to solve the problem can be found in Job chapter 2 just after God allowed the devil to take everything from Job that he valued. Job's three friends "sat on the ground with him for seven days and seven nights. No one said a word to him because they saw how great his suffering was."

Being a leader is lonely. Being a fallen leader multiplies that loneliness exponentially. Most of the people you considered friends have gone. Shame is at the forefront. Torment is constant. Regret and disappointment rule the day. Yes, they are consequences of sin for the fallen leader, but the community focus needs to be on reconciliation and restoration.

Presence means being there, letting a fallen leader know you care. Among all the loss in Job's life, his friends did nothing immediately but be present. They initially said nothing.

They did not initially come with answers to all of Job's problems. They surveyed the environment and chose to sit with him in silent support for seven days.

Job's friends used wisdom and were present for him.

But what if the modern fallen leader does not make themself available? This is possible because of their state of mind during a difficult time. They may be still living in delusion. Their head might still be spinning. They might just be getting a grasp of the reality of their situation, and their shame might be overwhelming.

Presence of mind.

You could send a card, or better yet, drop it off without saying a word. Send a text. Send an email. There are many examples of things a person can do that can show you are thinking of them. This brings great comfort to a person that is crushed, especially when they have been crushed by their own actions.

Acknowledging someone else's pain, no matter the cause or circumstance, is a universal provision of comfort. Dr. John Perkins said to me one time, "True compassion comes from entering someone else's pain." It's not always possible, for a number of reasons, that you can enter someone else's pain, but there is no question that you can acknowledge it.

Again, the focus is reconciliation and restoration.

You don't have to engage in debate over the situation with the fallen leader. You don't have to solve the problem. You don't even have to verbalize words of comfort. You can just let them know you are thinking of them and they have value.

In doing any of these things you are saying you care. Note what you are not saying: you are not saying that you agree with what they did. You are not supporting any of their sin or junk.

Sometimes our pride will not allow us to take action in a situation like this.

Even in the most pressure-packed situations full of hurt, anger, and disappointment, our job is to be faithful. Solving the problems and making all of the puzzle pieces fit is not our job; it's God's. It's here that the offended parties need to focus on obedience and pleasing God.

Sound impossible in the context of all the ugliness? It's not, as long as the focus is on God and not the offender or ourselves.

Most times a fallen leader won't expect you to condone what they've done, but they may be grateful that you continue to show them friendship. Or they may not. They may refuse you and turn you away. But with gentleness they may, even tentatively, agree to meet or stay in touch.

A person needs to be able to see beyond the person and circumstance in front of them and see God extending his arms and waving them toward Him, taking the offending party out of focus.

At this point in the life of the fallen leader it is your job to deliver to them what they need, not necessarily what you think they deserve.

Who knows? You may be God's special instrument of grace to them.

THE POST-FALL ROLE OF THE COMMUNITY: DOLING OUT CONSEQUENCES

The consequences of a fall are not ours to dole out, are they? The temptation to try to make the fallen leader hurt as much as each individual around them hurts is strong. The temptation for revenge is, unfortunately, human.

Now, that's not to say that naturally and in the course of recovery from whatever happened that an individual around the fallen leader will never be part of a consequence for that leader.

Might a spouse need to separate from their unfaithful partner for a period or longer? Possibly. Is it possible that the individuals on a board might choose to remove a leader from their position temporarily or permanently? Definitely. There may even be legal consequences.

But too many times the hurt and betrayal rise to such a level that those closest to a fallen leader are tempted to search for ways of forcing consequences on them. Instead of the focus being on restoration and reconciliation, the focus is on making the offender pay.

I am not letting the leader off the hook. But we all have a responsibility directly to God, not considering this particular situation or the circumstances of the hurt.

Allowing for the pathway to restoration to be clear can be difficult for those closest to a fall. A fallen leader may see the clear path, but that path can often be blurred by those around them who sometimes take on the role of doling out consequences. Unfortunately, this group often is made up of people the leader has hurt deeply and with whom they have a deep emotional attachment. This group can also contain people close to those most hurt who have taken up their cause.

This is another example of where the rest of the community and those not as close to a fall can really be of assistance to the fallen leader and those closest to them.

POST-FALL ROLE OF THE COMMUNITY: RESTORATION

I fully agree with author, speaker, and founder of Eternal Perspective Ministries Randy Alcorn when he says, "Repentance and Forgiveness always means full restoration to fellowship in Christ's body. It does *not* mean you should go right back into a position of leadership."[39]

In his book *Fallen Spiritual Leaders*, F. Lagard Smith writes, "We must abandon forever the notion that fallen spiritual leaders are irredeemable and expendable."

If a fallen leader is repentant, there should never be a question as to the commitment we have to restore them to fellowship. I don't even believe it is our job to deeply examine if their repentance is genuine. Again, not our job. In the name of Christ, the fallen leader should get the benefit of the doubt.

Skepticism from the damaged toward the fallen leader is a natural consequence of what they have done. But the fallen leader who only sees cynicism and skeptical attitudes toward them will struggle with discouragement and be tempted to give up.

The fallen leader who has repented and is truly attempting to get back into fellowship needs to see the pathway to making it happen. Cynicism and skepticism can throw up a roadblock.

No way am I saying the fallen leader should have carte blanche to do whatever they want, making everyone their doormat.

But we should always be willing to move forward with love and encouragement, which takes great courage and focus.

Sometimes that means we have to put ourselves aside. That is no different than the difficult ability to be obedient against human nature that we otherwise practice. Heck, if for no other reason, the last two verses in the book of James should motivate us: "My brothers, if one of you should wander from the truth and someone should bring him back, remember this: Whoever turns a sinner from the error of his way will save him from death and cover over a multitude of sins."

Humanly, that can be very difficult, but the goal must be restoration.

LEADER, MOVE ON

The fallen leader who knows they messed up and is working to repair what they have damaged has looked into the disappointed, teary eyes of those closest to them as they attempted to explain what happened.

This leader was at the top of their game by all accounts and now has a deep paranoia in walking down the street of their hometown or even attending church. This leader is so embarrassed by their actions that they struggle to leave home.

The ironclad credibility this leader once had was destroyed by one poor decision after another, and there are now few people who believe a word that flows from their mouth.

The fallen leader's mind plays terrible scenarios of where they will end up in their life. This person struggles to see relationships reconciled, restoration taking place, and perhaps even organizational survival.

I know this all firsthand. I once was this fallen leader.

The following sections are about encouraging a fallen leader who acknowledges the actions that have brought them to this place. They will help the leader reach a place in their own mind and heart that allows for repair, reconciliation, and restoration to the best form of person God can use them to be in His service.

Fallen leader, the following sections are written for you.

LEADER, MOVE ON: A MARKED SEPARATION

There is absolutely nothing you can do about the facts of what happened in the past—the hurt you hurled onto others or the hurt you experienced. But while working to repair the damage, you can draw a line in the sand and work to discern how God wants to use all of your junk to benefit Him.

God wants to use you and all of the trouble you have chosen, but you have to recognize the fall as a comma (a marked separation) in your life and not a period. Frankly, it was this recognition in my life that has me sitting here writing this book.

T. D. Jakes puts it this way: "When you begin to realize that your past does not necessarily dictate the outcome of your future, then you can release the hurt. It is impossible to inhale new air until you exhale the old."[40]

Cory Asbury puts it another way in his song "The Father's House:" "Failure isn't final when the Father's in the room."

God is knocking on the door. Are you going to let Him in the room?

LEADER, MOVE ON: USING YOUR JUNK

Pastor and author Jentezen Franklin once said, "Impossible odds set the stage for amazing miracles." And God is in the miracle business. You have no idea what miracle is being whipped up in your life.

It is entirely possible that the journey following your fall could propel you further than you could have ever gone in your own spiritual life. It is also possible that the impact you might have in the lives of those in your sphere of influence may be multiplied because of the experience of your fall.

Pastor Steven Furtick says that "your rejection in one season can lead to your destiny in the next."

Whatever you allowed to bring you down is a blip on a screen, if you allow it to be.

If you plan to play the victim and live in a world of despair where every challenge of life is related to what happened, then it won't be a blip. But like so many things, it is your choice. Accepting God's grace and forgiveness is your choice.

Don't let your fall form a period in your life.

Allow God to use it.

LEADER, MOVE ON: YOUR FALL, NO SURPRISE

As I've heard Dr. Bryan Chapell say, "Do you see that the Bible takes care to tar virtually every biblical figure but one?" God gave us a tremendous number of examples in scripture of imperfection that was used by God for His glory.

Most people reading this book will find familiar the stories of David, Joseph, Moses, Abraham, Peter, and Paul as examples of people who fell in scripture but who God used mightily.

All of them messed up, yet we are still learning from them thousands of years later.

I ask with reverence: Weren't there probably better potential disciples for Jesus to have chosen? Maybe, maybe not. It's not for me to judge.

But one thing I do know is that Jesus spent his time with the downtrodden, the imperfect, the religious, and the outcasts of society, and He used them for the advancement of the Gospel.

Sorry, but you and I fit much of that description.

God knew your human frailties and imperfections before you fell, just like those biblical heroes listed above.

He knew you were going to mess up but used you anyway.

He is God. He knew even before you were born, and definitely before you took your position or founded your organization that you were going to fall. He allowed it anyway because He has a greater purpose for your life.

While I will never minimize what you did or the damage you caused, the picture we have of it is very limited. Our line of sight is simply only human in its view. God sees the ramifications of your actions long into the future, and you must recognize that.

So, what are you going to do with all of that? Are you going to waste the pain?

I would recommend spending time in prayer, scripture reading, and meditation in order to determine how God wants to use your junk. But we have to set ourselves—our emotions and our pride—aside and allow for that revelation.

LEADER, MOVE ON: I'M STUCK

There are people that want you to remain stuck. The spiritual battle you find yourself in wants you to remain stuck. If you are stuck, you are making the choice not to allow God to use the pain of your former circumstance, the "sin that so easily entangles," for His glory.

There are people you may not even know that need to hear your story so what they are humanly feeling can be validated.

These people need someone to walk through their pain with them. Who better to do it than you?

You can do it! But you can't allow yourself to get stuck and focused on a temporary period of poor choices. The reason to push on and not get stuck may be much bigger than you or the temporary place you find yourself in.

Dr. Martin Luther King said, "If you can't fly, then run. If you can't run, then walk. If you can't walk, then crawl. But whatever you do you have to keep moving forward."

If you give up your fight, surrender, and choose to walk in God's direction, you will pick up skills that only your unique situation could have given you. God has spoken to you in unique ways, and you are commanded to pass on the skills and the comfort God has given you.

But it is only unlocked by giving up and surrendering your will to God's.

Again I say, leader, don't give up. Successful real estate and *Shark Tank* investor Barbara Corcoran has said, "Every single failure has an equally great upside if you are willing to stay in the game."

You have no idea what God has out in front of you that you cannot see, even if you messed up. Whenever I get nervous about the future and insecure about what God has out in front of me, I remember that He is already there waiting for me. I just need to be faithful in getting there.

LEADER, MOVE ON: THAT'S NOT YOU

Leader, this is probably the toughest period of your life. Although you may hate to admit it, the image other people have of you hangs heavy in your mind. You went from being everyone's hero to….well, let's just say you're not anymore. That's hard to take. You know you are a good person, but nearly every word that comes out of your mouth is fraught with ulterior motives in the minds of those around you. At least that is how it seems.

The vision people have of who you are is probably way different than the truth of your true identity.

When I was about 15, I spent a lot of time at the YMCA. I arrived one afternoon and ran about two to three laps around the track when a guy and his friend showed up on the stretching platform. Both of these guys were older than me; I would say in their 20s.

One of them was a skinny, scruffy guy in cutoff jeans and sneakers. The other guy was, let's just say, portly and wearing a similar outfit—hardly the athletic type. I stopped to talk and, as a young cocky athlete in the best shape of his life, started talking trash.

They would have none of that but kept their cool. The skinny guy said to me that the portly guy could run farther and faster than me. I looked at him and laughed. I took the challenge.

We agreed that we would run 40 laps, or two miles, to start out. If we were even at that time, we would do another 40, and so on until someone dropped out. It would be over if one of us lapped the other.

We started out even for about the first 25 laps. He was slightly behind me, but that was just because the track was narrow.

As we approached 30 laps, we got to the section near the stretching platform that was slightly wider, and he passed me. I was right behind him struggling for about five more laps, and then he took off.

His speed crushed me, and at 40 laps, he lapped me. Game over. I was so embarrassed.

Leader, you are beat up right now. You thought you were in the best shape of your life and, as author Steve Farrar puts it in his book *Finishing Strong*, "You got ambushed." Your focus was lost. Steve continues, "Your fall could have been the ambush of another woman, the ambush of money, the ambush of a neglected family." But you are not who you used to be, and you appear to everyone else to be completely out of shape, off the rails, and down for the count.

Who you know yourself to be deep down inside, especially considering your identity in Christ, is who you are.

The guy on the running platform that day knew he could run, and so did his friend. He just didn't look like it. I thought he looked like he should be sitting in his basement in his underwear eating cheese curls and playing video games.

Guess what? On the outside you may need to wipe the cheese off your mouth and fingers, but inside where the Holy Spirit lives and your identity abides, you are strong and able to outrun any judgmental and critical community around you in order to honor your commitments. The Holy Spirit gives you that power.

But are you going to do it? That is your choice.

God gave you this life because He knew you were strong enough to live it. He knew everything that was going to happen in your life. He knew your successes and your failures. But He gave you the life you have regardless. He gave you the level of influence you have anyway.

That potential to influence has not changed. The way that potential is to be applied possibly has changed.

Some people may be tearing you up, some may be sitting back and skeptically watching your every move, and some may be encouraging you to get back on your feet. But they are definitely watching. In fact, more people may be watching you than before your fall.

Some would call that an opportunity. I would.

Yes, it's going to take some time to get your head on straight and organize your thinking again. It is going to take some time to repair and reconcile relationships. It's going to take some time to start to build trust again. And the list goes on....

But never lose sight of the incredible opportunities that are in front of you:

1. The opportunity to impact even more people as they watch how you react.

2. The positive use of your experience as you encourage others.

3. The opportunity to show people they can be strong in adversity in Christ's power.

4. The opportunity to show people that you are not perfect, and they don't have to be either.

5. Most importantly, showing everyone that this is how God works in a Christian's life.

And that list also goes on....

It's *your* opportunity.

It's been given to you.

Take the opportunity and live it.

―――――――――――――――

A few years after my fall, and after going through many deeply painful and life-altering experiences, my closest friend of over 20 years wrote the following text to me: "I am sorry I have not been a better friend to support you. I can't imagine the pressure you must be under. I am praying that you will sleep well tonight. I was thinking that maybe you do feel trapped in the situation, but with God there is always a way out. Trust Him to guide you."

Not bad. Although I spent some time being angry and bitter about the way he initially reacted to my bad decisions (I considered him part of the legalistic first group), we are now back to being good friends. It took a lot for him to text me this sentiment, and I deeply respect it.

So, whether you are a board member, constituent, congregant, community member, or a good friend, who do you want to be when all of the dust clears? Is your leader, as a person, worth your effort? Is your organization worth it?

I know they are.

CHAPTER 10

WHERE TO FROM HERE?

YOU MADE IT to the last chapter. You've identified with something I've written on these pages, enough so that you probably recognize you have a role in helping to save a leader from a potential demise. You realize there are some difficult questions that you need to Courageously Ask.

Really, it doesn't matter what role you may play in the prevention of that potential demise; you could even be the falling leader yourself.

This book is the culmination of plenty of experiences and hard-fought victories by God and a group of fallen leaders, including me.

This book had a particular focus, as is stated in the subtitle: "A Proactive Approach to Prevent the Fall of Christian Nonprofit Leaders." This was definitely the focus, and I hope there will be a benefit to the nonprofits you find yourself involved in. But there was probably a side benefit.

While the focus of the book was on leadership and executives, all of the principles can be applied to all of the people around you. All people need encouragement, compassion, love, acceptance, and the ability to be who they are without fear. My hope and prayer is that God was speaking to you through these pages. These principles may help in your marriage, your family, your work relationships, your relationships at Church, and on and on…

"THE THINGS WE NEGLECT LEAD US TO A PLACE OF REGRET."

That is the same quote from Brendan Bridges of Richvale Church in California that I used earlier in the book.

During the writing of this book there were multiple Christian nonprofit leadership falls. The descriptions of them run the gamut, from popular celebrity preachers to well-respected international ministry leaders.

The main reasons for the leadership falls I am referring to were of a personal nature, similar to those addressed in this book.

Hindsight by the accountability structures around these leaders is 20/20 just like anyone else. Their oversight, and sometimes inaction, concerning the leadership of the organizations admittedly fell short and is looked on with much regret by the organizations.

Below is part of an open letter released to the public by one of the organizations:

> We now know based on the investigation that [our leader] engaged in a series of extensive measures to conceal his behavior from his family, colleagues, and friends. However, we also recognize that in situations of prolonged abuse, there often exist significant structural, policy, and cultural problems.
>
> That a leader under our care sinned against others so grievously pains us. We were trusted by our staff, our donors, and the public to mentor,

oversee, and ensure the accountability of [our leader], and in this we have failed. The findings of the investigation have caused us to take an extensive and humbling look at ways that we have fallen short, made mistakes, and failed to love well.

We regret that we allowed our misplaced trust in [our leader] to result in him having less oversight and accountability than would have been wise and loving.[41]

In other words, they did not Courageously Ask. Honestly, I could have chosen any number of statements from accountability structures after they have experienced a leadership fall.

Leader, accountability structure, community—this could be your statement if you do not consider a proactive approach to prevent the fall of a Christian nonprofit leader.

Do not neglect or take for granted the complete humanness of your leader. A fall could happen in your organization.

WHAT TO DO, WHAT TO DO?

You see opportunities in your organization, whether you are the leader, the follower, the board member, the subordinate, or the congregant. You hopefully have recognized that you, as the leader, are a fallible human being, and that's okay. Another group of you have hopefully seen that your leader is a fallible human being just like you, and that's okay too.

So now there is just one question to ask: What are you going to do about it?

I say that, knowing that throughout this book you have been able to see yourself in certain situations that you could have done better. I would bet you have even made a commitment (or several) to change some things and even reach out to those your inaction has affected.

The effort I have put forth in writing this book as an invitation to partnership in impacting our nonprofits is worth nothing without action.

This is where our efforts come together, and we become a team.

I have been transparent and have done my best to give you the tools to help you develop a proactive approach in preventing the fall of a Christian nonprofit leader.

Now you must take action. What you do right now could spur on a proverbial butterfly effect, with you never realizing the results of your action this side of heaven.

I hope you have come out of this book fired up and motivated.

God has a plan. Now it's up to you to discern what link in the chain you are.

THE LINKS

I founded a free, Christian health clinic as a vehicle for people to see Christ's love in action. It was, and still is, about human relationships.

I recognized early on in my Christian walk, and still believe today, that although God could make the path what He wants, people need to know you care about them before they will listen to what is important to you. The vehicle we developed to do that was the health clinic.

I remember there were people, pastors even, that would attempt to pressure us into aggressively sharing the Gospel during every visit no matter what. I did not go for that. Sometimes it was appropriate, but sometimes it was not. That high-pressure, in-your-face method was very damaging in my life, and I would not yield to those folks.

To me, it was all about relationships and expressing God's love first.

Whenever I would be challenged by staff or volunteers who had direct client impact, I made it very clear that their goal should be to figure out what link in the chain of a person's life they are. Until they developed relationships and got to know our clients, there was no way of knowing where the person truly was in their spiritual journey. Our staff was to assume nothing.

This caused them to listen to our clients to see where they were in their lives and gave our staff the freedom, devoid of pressure, to get to know our clients and love on them.

I would presume that God smiled down on this approach and is one of the reasons the clinic is very strong and growing their Gospel presence many years later.

So, what link in the chain are you in whatever context you find yourself? You could be on a board that is watching their leader fall, but not talking about it. You could be a leader who is falling, but doesn't know what to do. You could be on a board that has a strong leader who seems to be doing everything with excellence right now. You could be an onlooker seeing some peculiar things in your leadership. You could simply be around a leader who needs some encouragement and a "soul care" person.

No matter where you find yourself, your leader or organization needs action. That doesn't mean getting in their face and pushing them around. It just might mean a text of support or to let them know they are on your mind. It can be just that simple. You may also have some major decisions to make.

And you just might have to Courageously Ask difficult questions of yourself, someone you know, or the leader of an organization you care about. This could be the key in preventing a fall. My hope is that you have been encouraged to make it over that hump of doubt, and are prompted to take the next step. It's time to start a conversation.

APPENDIX: MY STORY
AS IT RELATES TO THIS BOOK

I HAD JUST gotten done telling my board of directors I was involved in a three-month emotional affair outside of my marriage. My wife found out after she looked at my cell phone records.

We were all jammed in my office at a table that was much too big for the room. The board barely fit around those two six-foot tables pushed together. It was uncomfortable to begin with. Then you add in the tension of the news just delivered, and it was miserable—at least for me.

It was a relatively small, but significantly growing, Christian nonprofit I founded only four years earlier based on a clear calling from God. God called me to impact a very difficult, poverty-stricken neighborhood in our city for Him, and the vehicle was a faith-based, free health clinic.

By this time we had served well over 1,000 clients and delivered over 3,000 visits. There were 15 medical providers and over 40 volunteer nurses and staff.

After I finished explaining everything, one of the board members looked at me and asked, "What part of your issue did [our organization] play?" It was something I had never thought about. The answer escaped me.

My only focus was that I had royally messed up, sinned against my God, betrayed my wife and my kids, and had let many people down based on one poor decision after another. In my mind, I accepted responsibility; I was accountable, and that was it.

I had no idea where that question from the board member came from, but it has haunted me for a long time and has been the subject of many conversations since. My findings, as I reflected on the question, are detailed all throughout the book you are holding.

This appendix is written to give you some background that led up to my fall and the origins of this book. You will find that some items in this appendix have been pulled and used throughout the book.

THE BIG READJUSTMENT

Prior to the calling to start the clinic ministry, I was involved in everything. My involvement was to the point it was probably sinful and misguided. I was a certified biblical counselor; I was organizing and running events; I was going on multiple mission trips per year; I was serving on multiple boards of directors; I was leading adult Sunday school; I was attending men's Bible study groups.

Do you see the trend here? Everything was "I, I, I, I, I..."

In fact, if something was taking place at church that I wasn't part of, it offended me. All of this was on top of a highly demanding management position, raising two kids, and trying to be a decent husband.

So, about eight years before the day in my office when I told our board of my transgressions, I began to be called to ministry.

I didn't realize it at the time, but I can see it clearly now. It started with being strongly impacted by a few sermons God used, which led to a meeting with my pastor, and finally moved into some books I was reading. These all formed the indicators of the call I was starting to receive and embrace.

The first message of conviction I heard was about loving and serving people without expectation of reciprocation. We've all received teaching like that in our lives, but for some reason God planted that message in my heart with purpose. I am a person of action, so I had to do something with it.

During this period, I met with my pastor because I found my personal ministry scattered, and I wasn't being as impactful for Christ as I would have liked. I also recognized my endeavors were becoming prideful. My service for Christ had gone down the classic path of being more about "doing" than about "being." And I could sense it. I needed to focus my efforts and get back on the humble servant train.

We talked about it for a while, and he recommended I read the book *Game Plan* by Bob Buford. I found this book to be excellent, and it definitely helped me to identify what God had uniquely designed and prepared me for. I highly recommend it. It identified my God-ingrained desire to help urban youth.

Because of the identification of what purpose God had specifically designed me for, I started to pull myself from boards that did not fit this design. At the same time, I answered the requests to be on boards that did.

One in particular was a board for a growing inner-city private school of about 200 children who were among our community's most vulnerable. Their families desired a solid Christian education, but for the most part did not have the resources to do so. I had previously been asked to check out this board by the founder of the school, but I was too busy and had put it off.

During one of the first meetings I attended, the founder gave out a book to each board member. The book was *When Helping Hurts* by Steve Corbett and Brian Fikkert. This was another influential work that went right along with God's calling on my life. The title is self-explanatory, but it taught me valuable principles around poverty and how we can truly impact the poor without unknowingly hurting them.

It was easy and natural for me to take these principles and run with them. Combine these principles together with the sermon on serving people without reciprocation and you have a formula for true service.

So, what did I do?

I picked out the poorest and most challenging neighborhood in my city, gave out peanut butter and jelly sandwiches and juice boxes for over two and a half years as I pulled a little red wagon through the streets. I was a balding 40-something white guy in shorts and high tops walking through a neighborhood that could have easily been a case study for the difficult challenges in urban culture and our cities. I stuck out but carried on in God's motivation and protection.

I determined to develop a relationship with this neighborhood without other agendas creeping in. The people in the neighborhood were skeptical at the beginning to say the least, but the relationships were built.

The second message I heard that affected me was a message concerning church unity. Not unity in our local church, but *Big C* church unity. I was convicted in a big way about this and began getting together with pastors around the subject. Many of the things I found were probably obvious to some, but not to me.

There are pastors out there who genuinely seek to work with other churches and recognize how God designed us to be one. There are also pastors who talk about church unity with grand passion, but when that unity will cost them something (not always cash), they back away from it. Then there are those pastors who are building their own kingdom according to their own agenda, with Christianity wrapped around it secondarily. By the way, I found all three of these groups to exist in the nonprofit world as well.

I started to pull together a diverse group of about nine pastors and churches I thought could come together to declare unity, put their desire for unity into action, and impact the community for Christ in a God-sized way.

Unfortunately, that never really formally happened. It didn't happen because my calling to the urban atmosphere derailed it, and it took a different form.

As I talked with pastors and community leaders about impacting the most vulnerable and church unity, I realized we needed to actually do something. I wasn't talking about an event that would come and go; I was talking about some sort of ministry that would fulfill a desperate need and show longstanding commitment to people in a struggling neighborhood of our city. I did not want to get bogged down in meetings. This was about action.

One of the major themes in *When Helping Hurts* involves developing strong credibility and relationship in the community before even mentioning Christ. In fact, the key to evangelism is relationship.

So what I was being led to do had to be a ministry that would:

- Fulfill a major need in the community while attracting individuals to Christ through solidly built relationships,

- Draw the Big C church together in unity, and

- Have an undeniable, long-term commitment to a neighborhood.

IMPACT ALL AROUND

During this period, my wife and I attended a small group Bible study with friends on Tuesday evenings. I had been continually telling the group about the incredible things God was doing in my life, the meetings I was having, the support I was getting, and the stories of handing out PB&Js in the city. I also started talking about moving convictions and ideas to action.

One Tuesday, as we were eating our snack before Bible study, the host (a physician's assistant) asked me privately if I ever considered a health clinic. I replied that I never contemplated it, but I would check into it and find out if there was a need.

Now keep in mind that until then I had zero experience in founding a nonprofit and most of my career had been managing grocery stores for a large chain and doing ministry. I knew nothing about starting and running a health clinic.

After a long period of measuring the need and gaining an invitation from the neighborhood association, the clinic opened about two years later with the same Bible study host being the silent cofounder and first medical provider. God provided the money (no government funding whatsoever) and expertise to make it happen.

Many churches from various denominations and community members came together to raise the funds, carry out a significant construction project, provide donations, create foundational documents, and construct a functioning clinical ministry. This ministry would honor God and lift up those who would need our services as we developed relationships with them.

And what had been developing inside me? I remember the first occasion I walked in the door of what would become the clinic and saw a local youth group starting demolition of the previous space. I teared up because the dream of my calling was actually happening.

I was humbled as I observed God doing things only He could do. The supernatural was taking place right in front of me. We say all the time that it is our responsibility to be faithful, and the rest is God's job. Here it was happening right in front of me.

While I cannot claim perfection, and there were things I would have managed differently as I look back, God was using all of it for His glory. It would be easy for me to tell story after story about things only He could have done.

But also, as I look back, I see God was not only taking an old building and making it new in His service, He was also taking the old me and transforming me into a much deeper disciple of His.

Once the clinic opened, we started serving the community. The opening yearly budget landed at about $70,000 with one part-time clinical coordinator, three very part-time volunteer providers, about 20 volunteers, and me. Over the next four years, the budget grew to about $240,000, one full-time employee, five part-time employees, one part-time paid medical director (the Bible study host), 15 part-time volunteer providers, about 40 volunteers, and me.

At that point we had served over 1,000 people! It was undoubtedly growing and thriving.

As a sidenote—at the writing of this book the clinic has grown to 3,000 clients and has provided over 11,000 patient visits. God is good!

THE CRACKS APPEAR

Our growth as an organization came with a lot of pressure for me. Whether others imposed it or it was imposed by me doesn't really matter; it was there.

We had to raise an increasingly large amount of support to keep it going. We now had employees, and we were serving more and more people, which takes money (we held strong to a policy of only accepting minimal government cash, less than 1 percent). We had incredible prayer partners, and God continued to provide for our needs.

But whether or not I realized it at the time, I began to struggle. It felt like a ton of people were counting on me to keep up the growth and would be disappointed if we didn't have a fresh program or event coming up. I would get a rise when I would share with someone about the new program or piece of equipment God was providing. You could see the excitement in their eyes, which became addictive.

All eyes were on me, and I watched my words and actions, making sure nothing I did would impact the clinic negatively. People continually spoke about the miracles God was working through me and told me how much I inspired them.

As I talked about new ministry possibilities, people started using terms like *visionary*. Some even mentioned I should run for mayor. While I know people tried to encourage me and lift me up, I had to be careful to not accept the credit myself, and eventually those well-meaning compliments created a lot of pressure.

I found this to be especially true within my own family. My wife, children, and other family members told me of how people were talking to them about what was going on, and they showed tremendous pride in the things God was doing through me. I remember my father-in-law pulling me aside and telling me how proud he was of me as he gave a hug. They all respected me immensely like they had never before, and I seemed to be their hero. Just what every person wants to be to their family, right?

However, all of this attention morphed into a standard I found impossible to humanly live up to.

I took the sacrificial gift of support very seriously. For example, I remember I became afraid to golf because one of our donors might see me and assume that was what I was doing with their money, creating a country-club lifestyle with their hard-earned cash.

When I dined in a restaurant I would scan the room to see who I knew and who I needed to talk to, if only to say hello. My world was all about cultivating relationships to raise the funds in order to keep the ministry growing, thereby increasing the influence and impact of the organization on the community. I felt like I had to wear the proper clothes, say the right words, and show up at the right meetings and community events.

As time continued on I no longer was myself, no longer the person whom God uniquely created to take part in what He was doing in the neighborhood that He directed us to. It became isolating and lonely.

The ministry slowly became my responsibility and not His. That was my downfall.

Needless to say, the troubles I was having as I dealt with the pressures of a growing nonprofit were brought home. The challenges and struggles of life and relationships were greatly exacerbated by the pressures, especially the growing pressures to not be myself. This is certainly a big part of our personal family story that is touched on in the book, but it is not necessarily the focus of this book.

The loneliness and isolation only became worse, as I could not be myself and tried to be perfect for the ministry and for everyone else, increasingly setting God aside. No one seemed to understand what I was going through.

During that time I reached out to friends, telling them I was struggling. Others now say they saw the signs of an impending fall. They didn't know what to do. I assume they figured I could handle it and would rely on God.

They had seen God work miracles in my life and through me in the form of the clinic, even though most of them initially doubted the call.

Why would I not be able to depend on God in the same way as I struggled? So they had mostly ignored the warning signs.

Eventually I no longer could survive in my pursuit to be perfect, and while dealing with the isolation of loneliness, I fell. After graciously giving me time off with pay to get things back in line, without much progress, the organization I had founded fired me.

A TOUGH TIME

There is no possible way I can accurately describe what happened during the next few years. Any attempt to do so would find me deeply hurting the people I cherish the most. As with any highly emotional experience of pain and hurt involving people, there are many perspectives.

No matter how I attempt to write what would be my best effort at an objective perspective, it would ultimately be my perspective. I'm not willing to take that risk.

I can assure you I am not avoiding my responsibility and accountability for my actions.

What I will do is try to encapsulate the main facts in a nutshell. Honestly, that may even be impossible.

After my fall, I initially fought almost everyone involved: God, my family, the organization leadership, and especially myself. I was getting nowhere. I stayed in town for months as I continued to battle my own demons, but I could not gain a foothold and was in a spiral as I felt continually attacked.

I moved to Washington, D.C. alone and got a job working with a grocery store chain. I filed for divorce.

At this point I was at the end of myself and trying to survive without jumping off the roof of my apartment building. That is not a flippant statement, and I mean it literally. The pain I had caused was excruciating and weighed heavily on me.

I could always feel God knocking on my heart, but I would not let Him completely take control like I had done previously. I look back and am amazed at His continual grace, mercy, and general presence in my horror of a life.

Over time, I fell under massive conviction, canceled the divorce, and eventually moved back to my hometown with my wife.

For those of you who lived this story, please forgive me for not validating in this section the depth of what you went through with details. It's not on purpose, but it would fall incredibly short, no matter what I would write.

HOW WILL GOD USE MY JUNK FOR HIS GOOD?

Once I got my head back on straight, this question became my focus: How will God use my junk for His good?

He does that, you know. He uses our junk.

A number of years ago, before the fall, my wife and I started visiting the Lincoln Theater campus of National Community Church (NCC) from our home in south central Pennsylvania, just less than a two-hour drive away. We would attend church on a Sunday and then ride our bikes around D.C. in the afternoon, returning home in the evening. We did this regularly.

We love the city, but what really motivated us to drive the distance and attracted us on Sundays was the high level of preaching at NCC anchored and led by Mark Batterson, the value they place on taking your faith outside the church to serve, and the diversity of the congregation. Plus my wife especially loved the worship music.

After the fall, while my wife and I were long into reconciliation, we were attending a Saturday evening service at the Barrack's Row campus of NCC in Washington, D.C.

This is a great venue for church because it is a quaint, old-style theater first opened in 1909 on Capitol Hill with less than 400 old seats, a perfectly slanted floor, a concession stand, and textiles on the walls.

There was something different about this one particular evening.

At first, everything about the atmosphere was the same, as we sat waiting in anticipation of the service beginning: we were sitting at the end of the row midway back like we usually did, the lights were dim as people talked around us, and the worship band was praying in front of the stage.

About halfway through the worship set something changed. That is when God spoke to me.

During NCC services I am typically very attentive, starting with the music. Almost every week I walk away inspired and touched by at least one principle or concept that I heard. It is always very captivating and motivating.

On this particular Saturday evening after the service, we chose to have dinner at Ted's Bulletin Restaurant a block down from the theater. In the normal course of conversation, my wife asked me what I thought about the church service. My answer was, "I have no idea what was preached."

I really didn't, and I gave it a good amount of thought. I explained to her that something happened in my mind and heart that took me out of NCC that evening. Now, it's not like I was floating above the city meeting God Himself as He directed me in how to change the world for Him (although that would have been cool). But He definitely spoke to me in His own way and gave me an assignment based on the experiences of my life.

This experience heavily impacted me! That evening I felt like I was in a trance as I was working out all the logistics and next steps in my mind as we moved on to dinner and drove home. I was focused, motivated, and excited in a big way.

By now I'm sure you have figured out what my calling and assignment was.

It was using all of the junk that I put everyone through, including myself, to help leaders, especially executives, and those around those leaders to start a conversation.

The conversation that was needed was centered on creating a proactive approach to prevent the fall of Christian nonprofit leaders.

I'm sure you recognize that there are tons of details that would not fit into this simple appendix. I am pretty open about the details of my experiences, so nothing is purposefully hidden.

All of the details could be a book in themselves. I tried to pick out the parts that would help you understand me a little bit, so the book has some background and perspective.

ACKNOWLEDGMENTS

TO GOD BE THE GLORY.

WAY BACK, OVER 35 years ago, when I was taking English 102 at York College of Pennsylvania, there was a Professor Lois Revi. I have forgotten what the topics of my papers were, but she challenged me at every turn. She asked incredible questions. Through those interactions and challenges, a lifetime enjoyment of writing had begun. I never graduated college or wrote professionally up until now, but the appetite has been there and is evidenced in the small writing projects I have done. Somehow she helped me understand that the objective reading, followed by constructive criticism, of what we write is invaluable. I don't know where she is in life these days, but I want her and her family to know that her legacy lives on. For example, in the pages of this book.

That legacy of asking good questions while providing constructive criticism, and my value of it, was rekindled in my life through the editors that worked miracles with my raw first-draft manuscript, which turned into this book. The editors that performed this absolute magic were brought together by a company I engaged named Book Launchers. I'm telling you, pure magic!

I faked Christianity until I was about 30, when there were some life challenges. At that time, Cathy Barshinger and her counseling team taught me how to apply scripture to real life and that God's word is sufficient. Somehow I never knew how practical God's word was/is before that. This formed the foundation for the rest of my life and this book. No matter how far I may have strayed, those foundations were never broken.

There were many people who contributed directly to this book and the message of it, including those who formed my leadership style and ability to communicate. There were people who were interviewed, people who encouraged, and people who cried as they relayed their message. There is no possible way I can list them all. Many were informal meetings where we discussed the topics of this book over breakfast, lunch, or coffee.

There was a group that stood above everyone and went the extra mile in helping me develop the message of this book in various ways (in alphabetical order): Aaron Anderson, Matt Carey, Trent Davis, Traci Foster, Jeff Kreuer, Jeff Marble, Larry Richardson, Brooke Say, Pete Seiler, and Jim Tyson. Some did not want their name mentioned in this section, and I have not. But I want to acknowledge them as well. You know who you are.

I also want to acknowledge those close friends who helped me through the struggle that became the source of this book: Ron Bagley, Walter Brooks, Matt Leininger, Jeff Packard, Craig Wolf, Ron Wollein, Kelly

Yost, and Tracy Young, plus a few previously listed. Some of these found their primary role in listening; some simply kept me sane, and most reminded me who I am in Christ without judgment. I'm thankful for them all. I would be remiss if I didn't mention my men's small group that meets at the YMCA in York, Pennsylvania, every Tuesday.

I want to thank the Board of Directors of Katallasso, Inc. who did their best with what I handed them. They carried on the health clinic part of the ministry God called me to under difficult circumstances. The clinic is doing very well today and has blessed a tremendous number of people in the name of Jesus. Well done.

I am putting this final acknowledgment at the end because I did not want it to color the other acknowledgments, although it belongs in the second position of this section:

My mother allowed my life to happen when she did not succumb to the pressures of having an abortion when she was pregnant with me at age 16. I love you and owe you a lifetime of gratitude. I'll leave it at that.

TOGETHER, LET'S
TAKE ACTION NOW
AND PREVENT THE FALL

 Download worksheets and additional resources designed to strengthen your organization and help you continue the conversation. **briankreeger.com**

 Order discounted bulk purchases of this book for your company, organization, or community. **briankreeger.com**

 Book Brian Kreeger for speaking and consultations. **briankreeger.com/contact** or **brian@briankreeger.com.**

 Join our email list and receive exclusive weekly blog articles. **briankreeger.com/contact**

Get more insights, including updates on Brian's next book about the aftermath of a fall.

 **/PREVENTINGTHEFALL** **/BRIAN-KREEGER-34347181/**

THANK YOU
FOR READING!

If you enjoyed *The Courageous Ask*, please leave a review on Goodreads or on the retailer site where you purchased this book.

ENDNOTES

1   "Do Christians Consider Their Pastors to be Friends?" Barna Group, October 8, 2019, https://www.barna.com/research/pastors-as-friends/.

2   "Ted Haggard," *Christianity Today*, accessed April 14, 2021, https://www.christianitytoday.com/ct/people/h/ted-haggard/.

3   Sarah Pulliam Bailey, "Megachurch Pastor Bill Hybels Resigns from Willow Creek after Women Allege Misconduct," *Washington Post*, April 11, 2018, https://www.washingtonpost.com/news/acts-of-faith/wp/2018/04/10/bill-hybels-prominent-megachurch-pastor-resigns-from-willow-creek-following-allegations/.

4   Kate Shellnutt, "Willow Creek Investigation: Allegations against Bill Hybels Are Credible," *Christianity Today*, February 28, 2019, https://www.christianitytoday.com/news/2019/february/willow-creek-bill-hybels-investigation-iag-report.html.

5   Steve Farrar, *Finishing Strong: Going the Distance for Your Family* (New York: Multnomah, 2000).

6   Farrar, *Finishing Strong.*

7   Iupui Lilly Family School of Philanthropy, "Giving USA 2019 Report: The Annual Report on Philanthropy for the Year 2018" (Chicago: Giving USA Foundation, 2019), https://lclsonline.org/wp-content/uploads/2019/09/GUSA-2019-AnnualReport.pdf.

8   William P. Barrett, "America's Top Charities 2020," *Forbes,* December 11, 2020, https://www.forbes.com/lists/topcharities/#5f3d1b3d5f50.

9   Tony Evans, *Kingdom Man: Every Man's Destiny, Every Woman's Dream* (Carol Stream: Focus on the Family, 2012).

10 "2021 Compensation Best Practices Report: Navigating Compensation in a Changing World," PayScale, 2021, https://www.payscale.com/cbpr.

11 Morgan Lee, "Richard Sterns is Leaving World Vision," *Christianity Today*, January 9, 2018, https://www.christianitytoday.com/news/2018/january/rich-stearns-world-vision-president-is-leaving.html.

12 "Most Pastors Feel Energized and Supported," Barna Group, October 3, 2017, https://www.barna.com/research/most-pastors-feel-energized-and-supported/.

13 Thuy-vy T. Nguyen, Richard M. Ryan, and Edward L. Deci, "Solitude as an Approach to Affective Self-Regulation," *Personality and Social Psychology Bulletin* 44, no. 1, (October 26, 2017): 92-106, https://doi.org/10.1177%2F0146167217733073.

14 Colin Wayne Leach, Naomi Ellemers, and Manuela Barreto, "Group Virtue: The Importance of Morality (vs. Competence and Sociability) in the Positive Evaluation of In-Groups," *Journal of Personality and Social Psychology* 93, no. 2 (August 2007): 234-49, https://doi.org/10.1037/0022-3514.93.2.234.

15 Jay E. Adams, "Motives," Institute for Nouthetic Studies, 2018, http://www.nouthetic.org/motives.

16 Glenn D. Reeder, "Let's Give the Fundamental Attribution Error Another Chance," *Journal of Personality and Social Psychology* 43, no. 2 (1982): 341–44, https://doi.org/10.1037/0022-3514.43.2.341.

17 Scott A. McGreal, "Why is the Fundamental Attribution Error So Confusing?" *Unique—Like Everybody Else* (blog), *Psychology Today,* August 13, 2019, https://www.psychologytoday.com/us/blog/unique-everybody-else/201908/why-is-the-fundamental-attribution-error-so-confusing#:~:text=Many%20laypeople%20confuse%20the%20FAE.

18 Mark Sherman, "Why We Don't Give Each Other a Break," *Real Men Don't Write Blogs* (blog), *Psychology Today,* June 20, 2014, https://www.psychologytoday.com/us/blog/real-men-dont-write-blogs/201406/why-we-dont-give-each-other-break.

19 Alice Boyes, "The Self-Serving Bias: Definition, Research, and Antidotes," *In Practice* (blog), *Psychology Today*, January 9, 2013, https://www.psychologytoday.com/us/blog/in-practice/201301/the-self-serving-bias-definition-research-and-antidotes.

20 Stuart Soroka, Patrick Fournier, and Lilach Nir, "Cross-National Evidence of a Negativity Bias in Psychophysiological Reactions to News," Proceedings of the National Academy of Sciences 116, no. 38 (September 3, 2019): 18888–92, https://doi.org/10.1073/pnas.1908369116.

21 Austin Perlmutter, "How Negative News Distorts Our Thinking," *The Modern Brain* (blog), *Psychology Today,* September 19, 2019, https://www.psychologytoday.com/us/blog/the-modern-brain/201909/how-negative-news-distorts-our-thinking.

22 Lauren Kent, "The Science of Gossip (and Why Everyone Does It)," CNN Health, May 11, 2020, https://www.cnn.com/2020/05/11/health/science-of-gossip-scn-wellness/index.html.

23 Thomas Saporito, "It's Time to Acknowledge CEO Loneliness," *Harvard Business Review,* February 15, 2012, https://hbr.org/2012/02/its-time-to-acknowledge-ceo-lo#:~:text=Nearly%2070%20percent%20of%20first.

24 Richard J. Krejcir, "Statistics on Pastors: 2016 Update," Churchleadership.org, 2016, http://www.churchleadership.org/apps/articles/default.asp?blogid=4545&view=post&

articleid=Statistics-on-Pastors-2016-Update&link=1&fldKeywords=&fldAuthor=&fld
Topic=0.

25 David F. Larcker et al., "2015 Survey on Board of Directors of Nonprofit
Organizations," Stanford Graduate School of Business, April 2015, https://www.gsb.
stanford.edu/faculty-research/publications/2015-survey-board-directors-nonprofit-
organizations.

26 "Board Recruitment," BoardSource, 2013, https://boardsource.org/fundamental-
topics-of-nonprofit-board-service/composition-recruitment/board-recruitment/.

27 Donella Wilson et al., "2018 Nonprofit Report | Board Governance: The Path to
Nonprofit Success," Green, Hasson & Janks Advisors (HLB International, 2018),
https://www.ghjadvisors.com/local-uploads/pdfs/Green-Hasson-Janks-2018-
Nonprofit-Report.pdf.

28 Cody Benjamin, "How Fast Do Downhill Skiers Go? A Guide to Lindsey Vonn's Best
Event," *CBS Sports*, February 13, 2018, https://www.cbssports.com/olympics/news/
olympics-how-fast-do-downhill-skiers-go-a-guide-to-lindsey-vonns-best-event/.

29 Jared Mellinger, "Self-Examination Speaks a Thousand Lies," Desiring God, June 7,
2017, https://www.desiringgod.org/articles/self-examination-speaks-a-thousand-lies.

30 "Statistics for Pastors." Statistics in the Ministry. Accessed May 5, 2021. https://www.
pastoralcareinc.com/statistics/.

31 "Board Engagement," National Council of Nonprofits, January 12, 2015, http://www.
councilofnonprofits.org/tools-resources/board-engagement.

32 Nancy Duarte, "Like Yoda You Must Be," Duarte, October 22, 2015, https://www.
duarte.com/presentation-skills-resources/like-yoda-you-must-be-2/.

33 Krejcir, "Statistics on Pastors."

34 "Do Christians Consider Their Pastors to be Friends?" Barna Group.

35 Andy Vaughn, "9 Ways to Support Your Pastor," Beliefnet, accessed April 14, 2021,
https://www.beliefnet.com/faiths/christianity/articles/9-ways-to-support-your-pastor.
aspx.

36 "Statistics for Pastors," Pastoral Care Inc., 2020, https://www.pastoralcareinc.com/
statistics/.

37 Joan Garry, "How Nonprofit Leaders Can Keep Their Organizations Afloat," *Harvard
Business Review,* April 21, 2020, https://hbr.org/2020/04/how-nonprofit-leaders-can-
keep-their-organizations-afloat.

38 Robert Niles, "Theme Park Cast Member Stories: The Day is Snowed at Disney
World," Theme Park Insider, December 7, 2009, https://www.themeparkinsider.com/
flume/200912/1577/.

39 Randy Alcorn, "Are We Shooting the Wounded or Acting in Love by Not Soon
Restoring Fallen Leaders Back to Ministry?" Eternal Perspective Ministries (blog),

September 6, 2017, https://www.epm.org/blog/2017/Sep/6/shooting-wounded-restoring-leaders.

40 T. D. Jakes, *Healing the Wounds of the Past* (Shippensburg: Destiny Image Publishers, 2011).

41 RZIM International Board of Directors, "Open Letter from the International Board of Directors of RZIM on the Investigation of Ravi Zacharias," RZIM, accessed February 2021, https://www.rzim.org/read/rzim-updates/board-statement.

e obtained